susie coelho's
everyday
styling

susie coelho's
everyday
styling

Easy Tips for Home, Garden, and Entertaining

Susie Coelho

Photography by Jennifer Cheung and Steven Nilsson

Simon & Schuster
New York London Toronto Sydney Singapore

SIMON & SCHUSTER
Rockefeller Center
1230 Avenue of the Americas
New York, NY 10020

Simon & Schuster and colophon are registered trademarks
of Simon & Schuster, Inc.
For information about special discounts for bulk purchases,
please contact Simon & Schuster Special Sales:
1-800-456-6798 or business@simonandschuster.com.

Designed by Jennifer Barry Design, Sausalito, CA
Layout production by Kristen Wurz

Manufactured in the United States of America
1 3 5 7 9 10 8 6 4 2
Library of Congress Cataloging-in-Publication Data is available.
ISBN 0-7432-1930-9

To Mom and Dad for your eternal love and inspiration.
I miss you both so much.

contents

preface

My Mother Made Me Do It

Thanksgiving Day. Fourteen years old. My mother had been slaving in the kitchen since sunrise preparing dinner for our family and about a dozen visiting relatives. Everything was on schedule until suddenly she realized that there was no centerpiece for the table. At my mother's table, the meal and conversation were always the main attractions, but Mom loved to add the little extra something that turned the special into the unforgettable, and a centerpiece would be just that touch. The problem was that there was gravy to be made and not enough of her to go around.

She handed me a pair of scissors and pointed me toward the door. I knew my mission: to comb the neighborhood for leaves, pinecones, twigs, branches, berries, and whatever else I could find, then come back and create something glorious for our holiday table within the twenty minutes left before the guests would arrive.

I went out foraging and returned with a garbage bag full of stuff. Without a clue how to make a centerpiece, I opted for free form. I laid the greens lengthwise down the table and then started adding dry leaves and pinecones. From time to time I stood back and looked at it from a distance, changing items according to my untrained but now involved eye. So far, so good, but it needed something else. I rummaged through a cupboard and found two old candlesticks and an Indian wooden horse trimmed in brass. With a candlestick at each end and the horse in the middle surrounded by clippings, I was finished.

The blur of motion that was my mother came to a halt.

"Sweetheart, that's lovely. I knew you were just the person to ask." The blur headed for the kitchen. "Now, please set the table."

By the next holiday, my eye was more discerning. I used all the experience and wisdom gained since Thanksgiving to create, if I may say so, an even better centerpiece. But my mother's challenges to my developing sensibilities had just begun.

Both my parents worked all week, so Mom designated weekends for putting the house in order. One Saturday morning during my sophomore year in high school I walked into the kitchen and found her staring pensively at the walls.

"I think a pale pink would be nice. . . ."

I tried to eat my breakfast as fast and inconspicuously as possible, but she finally seemed to notice me as I was slipping out the door.

"Honey, I'm going grocery shopping and to do some other errands."

"Okay, Mom. 'Bye."

"You paint the kitchen."

"What?"

"You can do it, honey. I know you can."

Despite my misgivings and my plans to spend the afternoon at the movies, Mom's encouragement and faith fortified me. If she thought I could paint the kitchen, I probably could. I actually began to warm up to the challenge. She handed me some money and pushed me out the door.

"Get a shiny paint, something that can be cleaned easily."

That was all the instruction I got. Around our house, there were no decorating magazines or interior design books to study, no time but the weekends to devote to the aesthetics of the home, and not enough extra money to hire someone else to do it. All my mother had was free labor—us—and an enduring desire to make the home a more beautiful and sustaining environment for her family. For us, it was always a matter of tackling a project quickly and having fun along the way. Mom was one of the early do-it-yourselfers, before there was even a label for it.

The kitchen turned out great, a subtle but glowing pink that cheered up everyone who walked into the room. Our house was like that—a warm and happy place. Mom decorated with an astounding array of objects—inexpensive and practical furniture from Sears, artifacts from her Indian ancestry, huge brass bowls filled with fruit, colorful artwork, pashminas tossed over chairs. The mix came alive with the things she loved.

My mother fostered in me a very personal sense of style in which there is no right or wrong, just the ravishing power of self-expression. And because she was such a firm believer in making the environment speak, she encouraged us to create, too. Little did she know that I would later make styling my life's work. Thanks, Mom!

My mother spurred me to create with a can-do attitude that has energized all areas of my life. Even when she didn't know how to do something, she tried. When she made mistakes, she picked up and moved forward. I learned that it's better to try than to be complacent, more meaningful to do something than nothing.

This simple, pragmatic approach still informs everything I do today. Though she wasn't trained or schooled in style, my mother taught me an invaluable lesson: By doing, I could gain the confidence to trust my instincts. Her spontaneous and heartfelt way of infusing her environment with beauty and love remains the core of my concept of style.

I invite you to share the blossom of the seed my mother planted.

Part 1:
Discover Your Everyday Style

1
Don't Wait— Style It Now!

2

**Open Your Style File:
The Spark to Get
You Started**

3

**Style File Binders:
Developing Your Vision**

Chapter

Don't Wait—Style It Now!

let's get going...

Lift Your Spirits with Everyday Styling

I recently drove up the coast to Santa Barbara on my way to visit my son, Hutton, on his weeklong camping trip with his school—ostensibly to check on him, but really because I miss him. The first year, his class went camping at Yosemite, and woke up to find me chasing bears out of the campsite with a few tin cans. This trip, however, stood double duty. We'd just finished moving into a new house and after all the hubbub of contractors and workmen from sunrise to sunset every single day, I needed a break.

My husband, Bobby, agreed to have some quality overnight dad time with our baby girl, Hailey, so I could take off to see Hut. I packed a few things, called my girlfriend Stina to make a date for dinner near her home in Santa Barbara, then jumped into my Navigator and hit the Pacific Coast Highway for a glorious drive along the coast.

After a relaxing dinner with Stina at the beach, we went to her Spanish-style spread in Hope Ranch, one of the most beautiful sections of Santa Barbara, where I was going to spend the night before proceeding on to Hutton's campsite at Lake Cachuma. As we walked in the door at 11:00 P.M., we were both bone-tired, but Stina wanted to show me her new white sofas. So instead of heading for bed we went to the living room where she went on to tell me that she was happy with the sofas, but didn't really like her glass coffee table; it seemed too modern, too stark. I agreed.

Of course, I couldn't go to sleep with this new challenge, so I asked her how her back was feeling.

"Why?"

"Because we're going to be moving a few things around."

Stina smiled in anticipation and we started with the first step of everyday styling: *clear your space*.

The first thing I was concerned with was the blocked entry to the seating area. You had to walk around two large chairs and a round table to get to the main sofa, and you couldn't see the beautiful stone fireplace. To open up the area for better flow and a more inviting effect, we simply moved each chair sideways and closer to the coffee table for a more cozy, intimate feel. I loved the round table and thought we could spotlight it better in the far left corner of the room as an end table between the sofa and another armchair. We tried it and it worked! On the

Style is not a secret code!

far side of the coffee table, two armchairs sat square to a small table in between—too rigid and formal, so I angled them out a bit. Ah. A much softer line.

We cleared the tables of magazines and other miscellaneous picture frames and artifacts.

Time so far? About fifteen minutes.

Now it was time for the second step of everyday styling: *gather your styling items*.

I asked Stina if she had any linens, extra pillows, pottery pieces, or candlesticks. She said everything she had was in front of us. "Tablecloths?" I asked. Just white or kitchen ones, she told me. Blankets, throws, fabric pieces? I was getting nothing but blank stares from her until I asked if there was something with a burgundy tint that would pick up the color in that pillow. Those must have been the magic words. She trotted off to a buffet in the dining room and pulled out a magnificent piece she'd inherited from her mom, a very old wool throw in burgundy paisley. I was knocked out, and she was thrilled at the idea of getting

some use out of this very special piece. We then collected a few other items from around the house.

Elapsed time: another fifteen minutes.

I couldn't wait to begin step three: *put your sense of style to work*.

Stina's jaw dropped when she saw that I was putting the throw on the coffee table. As I angled and folded it this way and that until it was just right, the stark glass table was transformed into a warm focal point and provided just the right backdrop to show off the beautiful vintage fabric. Energized by our styling success, we started adding candlesticks, books, and other items from around the room, trying things out and taking them away if they didn't work. I came across three burl wood boxes under the table. "I didn't feel they went anywhere," Stina said, but boy, did they! I quickly pulled them up and placed them on the table.

Finally, we moved some picture frames and a few accessories around in other parts of the room. Stina stood back and marveled. "Wow, it's a different room! I never would have thought to use those pieces that way. How do you do it?"

I reminded her that everything here was purely hers, things she'd collected, items she loved. I had only helped her by putting into play the three easy steps I'd learned from my own experiences, plus a little muscle. I reminded her there were many more styling items outdoors, such as flowering branches and wildflowers. If only it wasn't dark. . . . She bubbled with excitement. "I can't wait to go out tomorrow and pick up a few more pillows to match the throw, then hit the garden for some greenery for the living room." Now she was thinking like an everyday stylist!

We shared a big hug and both retreated happily to our rooms. Stina got a good night's sleep knowing she had a fresh new space to wake up to and a fun project to continue tomorrow. I slept soundly knowing that I'd helped her create her own sense of beauty and that our single spontaneous session had inspired her to *keep* creating. That's what everyday styling is all about. We didn't wait. We styled it now.

Putting It All Together

I first heard the word *stylist* when I graduated from having my mother cut my hair to being taken to an official beauty salon. The lady wielding the scissors, I was told, was a stylist. No wonder I got the wrong idea about what the word meant! Without so much as a single question, that woman gave me the fashionable cut of the day, then performed a bunch of magic tricks with gel and a blow dryer to make it look right. It never did again. Naturally, I came away thinking of a stylist as someone who might make you look great in the moment but didn't help you master the techniques to make the look your own. I couldn't go to the salon every day . . . so maybe I'd just skip style altogether.

Then I became a fashion model and met a different sort of stylist. In fashion-industry lingo, stylists are the ones responsible for pulling together the whole look of a photo shoot. They gather the proper wardrobe, the right shoes, jewelry and scarves, props such as furniture, flowers, food—everything needed to create the image the magazine, the client, or the advertising agency wants to put forth. As I worked on one shoot after another, I discovered that although the advertised product might be a simple yellow shirt and white pants, by the time the stylist was finished with me the picture could be a colorful scene straight from a Caribbean cruise, complete with brightly colored beaded necklaces, a scarf tied around my hair, and a huge floppy straw hat, finished off with cute multicolored sandals and a big red bag. Or—this is the critical part—the same outfit might be styled with brown leather loafers and a strand of pearls, a blue blazer over my shoulders and a white clapboard house in the background, and the statement was pure Cape Cod.

Now I started to understand. Style wasn't a thing, but a process—a creative fusion of elements that could completely change the way you perceived a simple yellow shirt and pair of white pants. It wasn't just the ingredients but the way they were put together that added up to style.

The seed planted by that impromptu Thanksgiving centerpiece years before began to germinate and soon I knew: I liked style. Styling was fun and it made me feel good. As I practiced it in my life and shared it with others, it became the creative yet practical process that I call everyday styling.

Everyday styling is about adding energy to space, creating the small touches that make the difference between a house and a home, a yard and a garden. You might add a strategically placed mirror to open up an area or serve as a dramatic backdrop to a piece of art. Soften the chandelier's angles by weaving vines through its tiers. Style the kitchen with a theme, set up a grouping of topiaries, or build a backyard bubbler. Styling allows you to accomplish mini-makeovers with maximum impact, bringing everyday pleasure and even a new perspective on life.

Both the process and the product of everyday styling are important. Together, they can make every moment more meaningful and fun for you and those around you. They light up your morning, inspire your day, deepen your evening peace.

You've got style. I'm going to help you to find it and use it to energize every aspect of your life, every day.

Why We Don't Style

If you've picked up this book, chances are that you feel your home and garden have some hidden potential you'd like to bring to light. You want to express yourself better in your space, but something keeps it from happening. Well, join the club. We're all multitasking like mad, commuting farther, working harder, parenting better, juggling more. Who can worry about the look and feel of their home when so many other things scream for attention?

My answer is, who can afford not to? We only get so many years on this planet. Are you going to let them pass you by without getting in your groove and making your mark?

Now you've zeroed in on the key word, *afford*. Doesn't it cost a lot of money to style your home? Isn't this a pursuit for the leisure class?

Absolutely not! Everyday styling is about making more out of your resources, and in the chapters that follow, you'll find lots of great low-cost ways to add luxury and flair to every square foot of your space. You can furnish a fantastic home with a few good trips to stores such as Target, Lowe's, or your local flea market for great styling finds at low cost. I still have a wing-back chair that I bought used for $25; covered with a throw, it continues to add an amazing aura of elegance to my bathroom.

Okay, let's say cash is not a concern. The real problem is time. No magic wand in the world can put more minutes in a day.

Poof! Just watch. The golden rule of everyday styling: The more you do, the more you *can* do. Improving your surroundings increases your energy, creating a natural buzz that fires up your drive better than a double latte. Too many people out there now are advising that we shrink our lives down to a diminutive size. It may be radical, but I say *expand*, don't contract! Maximize the moment! Make a mess! It's perfectly okay to be busy if all the activity is devoted to building the life you want and getting the best. Everyday styling is an energizing experience that enables you to make more of your time and pursue your goals with zest. Whether it's workplace performance, finding love, or nurturing your family, everything comes easier when you adopt the expansive approach to life that everyday style embodies. You have every minute of your life available to make it what you want.

Fine, but why not just go out and hire an expert and spare yourself the learning curve? Excellent point! I wouldn't be writing this book if I didn't think an expert could help and that you deserve access to the very best experience and knowledge available. But who wants to live surrounded by someone else's aesthetic?

Style is a personal process. An expert can guide your journey, but you've got to do the traveling. I've written this book as your guide. As a lifestylist, my charge is to help you develop and trust your instincts in creating the space you need to lead a fulfilling life. One that expresses your essence. One that makes every day a new opportunity to be . . . well, you.

Keep Creating

Tastes and needs change. Style never stands still. Everyday styling is a creative response to the changes that life naturally brings. It's an attitude of engagement, a personal embrace of change. And it's easy.

Tired of your sofa? Move it and change the pillows. Has the bedroom gone dead? Light it up with candles arranged on a mirrored tray to reflect the glow. Does the kitchen seem dingy? Spend an afternoon painting it a nice bright color. You definitely need to rearrange the furniture after a relationship breaks up to get a fresh start, and you might celebrate a personal success with a great new piece of art that provides an excuse to move everything else around. The changes in your life should be reflected in your space, and everyday styling makes it a natural process.

Then there are the big turning points. For me, becoming a mom altered everything. After years of elaborate entertaining, having a baby seriously simplified my lifestyle. I kept on giving parties, but the pâté gave way to potluck with friends bringing their favorite dishes. I armed my light-colored sofa with slipcovers and more rugged furniture replaced the antiques in the play area. My space, once designed for dancing till dawn, was rearranged for spreading out toys and chasing a toddler.

Everything you need to style your life is already within you. This book will help it to emerge. You don't have to read it straight through or take on everything at once. If springtime has you hankering to hit the garden, go directly to part III and get started. If you've been dreaming of a more romantic bedroom, head for chapter 6. You're the driver; I'm just the guide. Enjoy the ride!

Simple Guidelines of Everyday Styling

- **Experiment and try something new every day.**
- **Use common objects in uncommon ways.**
- **Tackle one small project at a time.**
- **Shop multiple sources, from unique boutiques to garage sales, thrift shops, swap meets, flea markets, discount stores, and the chains.**
- **Mix new and old. The old adds ballast and connection to the past; the new brings life, growth, and edge.**
- **Buy only what you love and watch your personal style emerge.**
- **When your house speaks, listen.**
- **Add, delete, move, change; make those pieces or plants work!**
- **Don't give up! Keep creating until you get what you want.**

Open Your Style File:
The Spark to Get You Started

2

focus and pull...

Creating Your Personal Style File

I promised you'd *do*, and now's the time to get to it. Where on earth do you start when it comes to styling your space? I begin with images and possibilities, a palette of options to choose from—what I call a Style File. Your Style File is an organized collection of pictures from magazines, paint swatches, fabric samples, and other visual cues that help you home in on your personal sense of style and bring it to life. By exciting and focusing your mind's eye, the Style File makes everyday styling a whole new way of seeing the world.

Why Start Your Style File?

Perhaps you look at your living room and think, "There are so many looks to choose from, which one is *me?*" Boy, is that the million-dollar question (sometimes almost literally)! The downside of living in an age of abundance is the confusing array of consumer choices. Not only do retail chains have signature product lines, each promising to be your style salvation (think of Pottery Barn and Pier 1, Ikea and Ethan Allen), but there are as many style subcategories, such as "traditional," "contemporary," or "country," as there are adjectives in the dictionary. (Are we talking French "country" or Tennessee "country"? "Traditional" as in a vintage gentlemen's club or "traditional" as interpreted by Ralph Lauren? The kind of "contemporary" you see in Hollywood movie penthouses or the twenty-somethings' take on today's fads that you find in first apartments?)

Every day, we receive mountains of catalogs and see millions of dollars' worth of television ads, billboards, and Web banners. Every time we open a magazine we get advice on how to dress, decorate, eat, and even breathe. There's lots of wonderful merchandise and talented people setting the trends, but at the end of the day, your home can only be your own if you give it your personal touch.

The Style File is designed to help you take control of media messages and make your own decisions. As with any decision-making process, the key to zeroing in on your style is to break down the problem. The Style File helps you (1) survey the available options, (2) assess the appeal of each alternative, (3) identify the elements that speak to your sensibilities, and (4) find out what fits into your everyday life. This process delivers a double payoff: not only will your Style File help steer you to the styling tips in the book that interest you the most, but it will also help you put your personal signature on all your styling projects. With a clear picture of the possibilities and your perceptions, you can begin to understand and express your own individual sense of style.

Some of you may want to skip ahead to try out some of the styling tips in parts II and III right away. But I do recommend that you get started on your Style File, whether now or after you've tried a few styling projects, to gather the idea bank that will make everyday styling a truer expression of you.

how the style file works

Your Style File is a place to assemble images that give you a styling spark, simply by gathering pictures from different places and bringing them together in an orderly way. In this chapter, we focus on the collecting process, which is something like procuring the ingredients for a recipe. In the next chapter, you'll learn how to turn your collection into decisions and vision—like cooking up a delicious dish.

Starting Your Style File

1. Set Up Your Files and Folders

2. Tear and File

3. Size Up and Sort

1. Set Up Your Files and Folders

First, designate a place for your Style File—a file cabinet drawer, portable file box, desktop file holder, or an accordion file that can hold several folders. My Style File is a portable wicker file box. I can put the box on the floor by my bedside table if I'm pulling pictures before I go to bed, or move it to the bathroom where I often end up with a pile of pages on the floor as I toss them out of the bath. Next, take four different color file folders. Label your folders "Indoors," "Outdoors," "Holidays," and "What Were They Thinking?" These will form the four main categories of your Style File.

2. Tear and File

Now, gather an assortment of magazines and catalogs that cover lifestyle. Start with your favorites, but you may also want to expand your possibilities by stopping at the newsstand and browsing for different looks. Ask friends and neighbors to pass on their old magazines to you instead of tossing them out. You'll save money and trees, and perhaps come across some new views. Socially minded style-filers might want to get together with one or more friends to do this exercise. You can share magazines and impressions as you go.

Flip through your magazines and tear out any page that shows something you like or that strikes you as stylish. We'll call these pages your "tear sheets." Don't overthink the decision to tear, just go with your first impression, your gut reaction, your instinct. At this stage we're talking *sensibility*, not sensible—so don't worry if you couldn't afford your dream kitchen in a million years. You might not even like the overall look of a room in a photo you linger over, but if an urn, a color, or a texture has caught your eye, go ahead and grab it.

By the way, if you're Web-savvy you can also surf shopping and home-decorating sites and print out images you like. A color printer helps these pictures pop on the page.

Here are some hints on what to look for as you flip and tear.

Indoors: Colors, textures, patterns, furnishings, textiles, lighting, accessories, space, arrangements, themes—anything from a specific item or characteristic to an entire environment or feeling. Don't limit yourself to the focal point of the photo. For instance, you might find just the right lamp for your study tucked into the corner of an ad for a bed.

Outdoors: What style of garden are you drawn to? Formal, colorful, overgrown, whimsical? Also look for a color palette, and the particular plants, trees, and flowers you like. Don't forget water features and other architectural elements, as well as pots and garden collections.

Holidays: Look not only for holiday decorations but also for recipes and menus, party layouts, holiday tables, gift wrap, and so on. Styling for special occasions becomes much easier when you have concrete ideas to get you started.

What Were They Thinking?: This is the file for pictures of rooms, decorating ideas, or objects that strike you in a negative way—things that turn you off, seem overdone, too stark, or look like odd mixtures. Style is defined as much by what you don't like as by what you do, and tracking the "no's" can help you to feel more confident about saying "yes." It can also help prevent expensive mistakes.

Identifying Your Personal Taste

As you tear out each page, take a fine-point marker and jot down the date in the upper right-hand corner of the page so that you can keep track of your taste over time. Circle what drew your attention to the page and make a note about what you like: "fun water feature for garden," "love this style of chair for kitchen," "outdoor lights nice for the winter holidays," "great green" (as your eye wanders to the color of the paint on the walls in an ad for a kitchen sink). Whatever it is that jumps out at you from the page, mark the spot. Every page will tell you something, and your job is to talk back.

Do the same for the What Were They Thinking? file, but this time note what it is specifically that you don't like. After you mark each page, file it in the appropriate folder. By the time you finish this part of your Style File, you'll already be gaining confidence in your own unique viewpoint and ability to identify your personal taste. Yes, your magazines will be torn to shreds, but your sense of style will be starting to come together. As you harvest images and organize them into groups, you're creating working files you'll refer to again and again. This is the palette from which you'll paint your vision. Can you feel your style coming to the surface?

3. Size Up and Sort

After you've spent an afternoon or a few hours over several days collecting images, you should have three full Style Files. (I don't insist that What Were They Thinking? be full—you'll have your whole life to add to that one!) The next step is to sort your tear sheets into more specific rooms or areas of your home and garden.

Before you start to sort, make a place for each section in your file box. Take four hanging files and label the tabs as you did your initial folders: Indoors, Outdoors, Holidays, and What Were They Thinking? Next, make up individual folders for each section according to the categories below. For some indoor rooms and outdoor areas, you may have more than one folder. (I like to use manila folders for Indoors, green for Outdoors, and red for Holidays.) *Note:* You don't need to sort What Were They Thinking?, so you can just slip that folder into its hanging file right now.

In the Indoors section:

- Living Rooms
- Dining Rooms
- Kitchens
- Bedrooms

- Family Rooms
- Entertaining Areas
- Breakfast Areas
- Bathrooms

(continued next page)

In the Outdoors section:

- Entrances (front, side, back)
- Kids Areas
- Seating Areas
- Entertaining Areas (patio, porch, deck)
- Garden (plants, flowers, accessories)

In the Holidays section:

- One folder for each of the holidays you like to celebrate, from Thanksgiving to the Fourth of July; Passover, Kwanzaa, Christmas; Valentine's Day, Halloween, Chinese New Year—any occasion that warrants dressing up your space

To sort each section, take one of your original Style File folders. On each page you should have a date, a circled area, and a notation of what you liked about it. Now look at the photo again and this time mark on the page what room or area this might pertain to—"orange for kitchen walls?" "good vine for trellis in side yard," "gorgeous holiday table," "great bedding for kid's room." Maybe you already noted a target room the first time. In either case, file the tear sheet in the relevant folder.

Replace the sense of uncertainty

Exercise: Focus and Pull

If you're having trouble finding photos with style that appeal to you, try this exercise to focus your search.

- Decide upon one room or area on which to concentrate.

- Take four index cards or pieces of paper. Write the answers to each of the following questions, one per card:

  1. *How do you want to live in this space?*

  2. *What feeling do you want this space to have?*

  3. *What are the colors that might create this feel for you?*

  4. *What collections would you like to spotlight here?*

- Lay the four index cards on the table or floor and go through your magazines again. When you see pictures that include an element of one of your answers, look it over more carefully. For example, if you've decided that the space is going to be a family eating area and gathering place, look carefully at that representation of a kitchen/dining room area. Maybe the way the throw rug is positioned under the table gets your attention this time around.

Your Working Style File

Don't be alarmed if you end up with a large file for kitchens, for instance, and nothing at all in porches. It probably just means the kitchen is higher on your styling priority list at the moment. Likewise, go ahead and file that single bathroom photo even if you don't expect to get to it for another year. You never know when the image might inspire you to pick up the one item that sets the styling in motion.

That's your Working Style File. You've replaced the sense of blank uncertainty that can stall even the most enthusiastic stylist with a rich catalog of creative ideas, all of which reflect your individual style.

Follow this same step-by-step process as you add to your Style File in the future, first filing photos by the four main sections and sorting them into specific spaces later. This two-stage approach frees up the process of pulling pictures, leaving the analysis for later so you can let your instincts go and your creative juices flow.

The spark of your style is captured. Are you ready to see it ignite?

While assembling your Style File, I bet two or three ideas really ignited a small fire in your imagination. Let's fan the flames. Pick a look that applies to a small area—a table, a corner of the room, a windowsill—and see what you can do with it. Using only what you can lay your hands on around the house or nearby, style that small area until it dances with light.

with a rich catalog of style ideas.

Style File Binders: Developing Your Vision

the big picture...

Bringing Your Style File to Life

Decisions, decisions—often so tough in the abstract but much easier when you tackle them with a vision in mind. Vision is important to achieve anything in life, and your Style File can serve as your source.

An image from my own Style File recently brought me a happy surprise. Soon after my daughter, Hailey, was born, I came across a photo of a bedroom that showed striped pastel walls and a wonderful carved French daybed. What a perfect Princess Room for Hailey, I thought dreamily. I pulled out the picture and added it to my Style File. Later, I played around with some fabric swatches in colors I thought might work well on the walls and windows. When I hit on a great combination I stapled the swatches onto the page and labeled it "Hailey's Princess Room."

Then reality struck. We were in the process of moving to a new home. Time and money were tight and Hailey was just a tiny baby. So, into the baby's room went what I had—a crib handed down from my son, Hutton, a pine armoire, some flea-market finds, and a queen-size mattress and box spring on the floor for sleepyhead Mom.

With the picture of the bed and its accompanying colors filed away, I tried to put the whole thing out of my mind. Where would I find this beautiful bed, anyway? And if I did, wouldn't the price of such an antique be prohibitive? Case closed. Still, the vision of the Princess Room bubbled away beneath the surface of my subconscious mind.

A few months later, scouting photo locations, I walked into a room and there was the bed! I stood and stared for a moment, unable to believe my eyes, then turned to the owner and blurted out the whole story.

"It's a little too small for our guests," he told me, "so it happens to be for sale." The price, it turned out, was no more than for a new bed. I bought it on the spot.

This is the power of a visual image: When you can *see* what you want, deciding how to get it becomes a natural next step. Thanks to my Style File the picture of my princess bed was so clear in my miind that I didn't hold back my admiration, hesitate when the owner offered to sell, or have a moment's remorse when I brought the bed home. Each step was joyful and easy because of the vision dancing in my head.

In this chapter, you'll use the images in your Style File to experiment, explore, and develop a clear picture of your vision (perhaps in infinite variations). You'll learn a unique way to play with styling ideas that makes anything possible and lets you take missteps on paper before they become expensive disasters in your home or garden.

If you started your Style File as described in chapter 2, you now have a file box of folders, divided by rooms and spaces, filled with images ready to go. By combining these cues with colors, textures, and forms, you can see individual images fuse and your inspiration become vision. Decisions follow as naturally as flowers in spring.

Developing Your Vision

1. Set Up Your Style File Binders

2. Select Your Favorite Images and Gather Styling Supplies

3. Mix, Match, and Experiment Until Your Vision Becomes Clear

1. Set Up Your Style File Binders

Equip yourself with three two-inch or three-inch loose-leaf binders. These can have a special look if you like. Fabric-covered, plastic neon, or perhaps three different colors for instant identification. *Tip:* If you pick the same color binder for all three sections, label them clearly or color-code them with colored ribbons. I like to do mine in simple brown paper because it reminds me of how I used to cover my binders in high school. I can color on them, make notes, draw, doodle, write an inspirational quote, anything I like. And when there's no more room, I can tear the covers off and start new ones.

2. Select Your Favorite Images and Gather Styling Supplies

With your binders at the ready, grab your Style File.

Go back through your tear sheets and pull out the ones you want to work with now—the images that inspire you the most or those that speak to a specific styling area. In fact, choosing one space to start with—perhaps the place that tops your project list—is a great way to focus your first experiments.

As you browse through your files, see if you can spot any unifying themes. Maybe you've always bought and planted annuals because that's what you know how to do but, lo and behold, the Garden folder of your Outdoors section is chock full of photos of cacti and exotic grasses. If so, I see some southwestern styling in your future. If the Fall folder of your Seasonal selections is particularly fat, you may have a taste for the feel and colors of autumn. As you identify such trends in your sensibilities, write them down on notebook paper and add them to the binders.

For any given space, narrow down your selection of tear sheets to six or so that represent your favorite style picks. Editing can help you make decisions. Slide your selected tear sheets into the plastic pages of your binders by section, one tear sheet for each side of the page.

Now, gas up the car because we're going to take a little ride. Gathering additional supplies is next on your styling agenda. Got your binders? Let's head for the stores—but you can leave your wallet at home. Today, we're strictly in search of free samples.

At the fabric store, browse around for colors and textures you like and ask for samples of materials you like. Most stores will let you cut small samples off the bolt. However, if they don't, you can either buy half a yard if it's a fabric that you love, or use paint samples and magazine tears for your color swatch. You don't need to have a particular use or room in mind; just follow your eye to the fabrics that make you feel good. Next stop is a paint store or two where you can collect color sample cards, thinking not only of repainting walls but also of redoing a wooden table, stenciling a chair, or using the sample to stand in for a curtain, carpet, or upholstery color. There's no charge for paint cards and they're invaluable for visualizing your styling ideas. Load up.

On to the furniture, carpeting, flooring, and tile stores. Believe it or not, many of these retailers have samples that can be carried away. Don't be shy! Look everything over and ask for samples of colors or patterns that appeal to you.

Stalking Samples for My Red-and-Cream Theme

My tear sheet shows a table with two tablecloths layered on top of one another, both of the same color palette but with different prints. Behind the table hangs a drape that repeats the same colors in yet another print. I love the deep reds and creams together—very warm and appealing—and I have a glimmer of an idea that this combination might be nice in my living room. Time to gather samples to put my idea to the test.

At the paint store I pick out paint chips to go with the red, one a shade lighter and another on the darker side. Oh look, there's my cream color. Grab it and go.

At the fabric store I'm on the lookout for fabrics with the same feel as those in the photo. I pull all the similar swatches I can find in solids, prints, and stripes. Even though I wasn't particularly looking for stripes, the colors are right, so I don't censor myself in the store. I never know what I might discover when I get home!

3. Mix, Match, and Experiment Until Your Vision Becomes Clear

With your images selected and your samples assembled, it's playtime!

Experimentation is the essence of the styling process and, as with anything, practice makes perfect. Experimenting with your Style File costs nothing and pays off in helping to develop your vision—and a whole new world of possibilities. Perhaps you'd like to mix prints without the risk of finding out that they clash *after* having the couch recovered. Maybe you've always wanted to splash your kitchen with orange and lime green but can't picture it as anything but white. Or it's time to paint the garage wall, but you don't know what color will go with the cushions on your patio furniture nearby. (See page 199 for Paint Board tip.) Your Style File lets you experiment—to look before you leap.

To get started, take one of your selected tear sheets from your binder and cut out the specific idea you like. Place it on a piece of 8½" x 11" white paper. Now lay your fabric swatches and paint samples this way and that on the page, mixing and matching until you come up with a combination that generates your styling smile. Staple everything into place, write any notes right on the page, slide it into a plastic sheet protector, and file it in the designated section of your binder. Now, whether you want to pursue that particular project or continue building on your idea with other tear sheet images, your vision is on paper and on file.

Don't forget to think outside the box as you work with your Style File. A snippet of flowered fabric might suggest a look you'd like to achieve in your garden. Paint cards can represent not just paint but colors for pillows, drapes, cushion covers, and plants. This is a game with few rules, except that you toss what you don't like and file what you do, so you can find your vision again when the time is right.

Continue this process of pulling tear sheets, gathering samples, playing with different juxtapositions, and filing the results in your binders by section. Keep the tear sheets you don't select for the binders in the original Style File folders for later.

Exercise: What Were You Thinking?

Come on, admit it. Somewhere in your house there's a monstrosity—a vase, cushion, knickknack, or wall hanging (all right, so it was a gift)—that thumbs its nose at all your efforts to style. Go—right now!—and kidnap the little troll. But don't throw it out, just banish it to the attic or garage, wherever you keep your styling supplies. Deleting the negative can be one of the most effective—and least expensive—styling techniques.

Your Portable Style File

A while ago, Bobby and I agreed that we needed new patio furniture. Our old furniture was given to us by my mother-in-law when she redid her home, and one day the webbing finally gave out. When I called about replacing it I found it would cost a cool $500 per chaise. "I don't *think* so," I thought, and sent half of it off to a charity thrift store.

Then one day, while pulling tear sheets, I came across a picture of furniture just like ours in a magazine and I shrieked as I realized it was now chic—collectible '50s-era outdoor furniture known as "mid-century modern." With a label like that I knew it must be worth something now, so I called a store that sold '50s and '60s furniture in Palm Springs. The owner was thrilled to purchase the items—and I was even more excited because it meant I had money to buy new patio furniture!

Cash in hand, I packed the kids into the car on a Sunday and took off for the one-hour drive to the beach, where I had seen the perfect

You'll have inspiration and

wrought-iron patio furniture for my new Spanish-style house. I decided to leave my husband at home, as he gets grumpy if he has to shop for too long or hear me constantly ask, "What do you think? What do you think?" I was so looking forward to my purchase and letting the kids run on the sand afterward that we just jumped into the car and zoomed away.

"Uh oh," I thought an hour later while staring at the handsome but *big* furniture and trying to re-create the size of my patio in my mind to figure out if it would all fit. In my haste to hit the road I hadn't stopped to measure the patio before I left, so with no written dimensions to work from, I circled my quarry, staring and calculating from every angle, asking utter strangers their opinion regarding the size of this furniture versus that of my patio, determined that if I thought hard enough I could control the physics of objects in space. Finally, my eleven-year-old son, who had been patient as a saint, said, "Mom, just go home and measure."

It was very sound advice. No lightning bolt was going to strike and burn my patio's dimensions into the ground. Disappointed, I drove home, my full wallet heavy in my pocket, and added all the important

measurements of my home to my Portable Style File as soon as I walked through the door.

I've been caught out on the road without the styling info I need too many times and have learned the hard way how being unprepared can squash the keenest intentions. Have you ever congratulated yourself on finally getting to the hardware or home store, only to realize as you stare dumbfounded at the display that you have no idea what the dimensions are for the thing you came to buy? What a frustrating waste of time! Or you're on the way back from the grocery store and see a garage sale, take a quick detour and discover a true treasure: an amazing quilt you want to toss over your couch, but you're not sure whether the colors are quite right to match the rest of the room. Rather than risk it, you drive on home. What a missed opportunity!

Everyday styling is an ongoing process often propelled by the inspiration of the moment—and where are you more likely to be surprised than when out on the road? Styling ideas surround you, and you need to be prepared. That's where your Portable Style File comes in.

As simple as a small notebook and a few add-ins that you carry with you when out and about, your Portable Style File helps you take your styling eye with you everywhere you go. Refer to it when you wonder if that sofa pillow's stripe is the right green or whether the little table you see at the flea market will fit in your bathroom. Think of every excursion as a styling reconnaissance mission and you'll be amazed how your resources expand.

Your Living Library of Style

From folders to binders to the notebook you take on the road, your Style File is a living library of your personal tastes, the practical reference and creative resource you turn to for inspiration and fire, your wellspring of vision and decisions. Remember to clean everything out once in a while, tossing images that no longer suit your sensibility, and to seize every opportunity to add new ideas and explore their possibilities. Congratulations! You're styling now!

your portable style file

To create your Portable Style File, pick up a small note-book and fill its pages with dimensions for any space you're working with, items you're looking for, and ideas for scouting styling supplies. Staple or glue in pictures, color samples, and snapshots of anything that might aid snappy shopping decisions. While you're out, collect notes and business cards from home and garden shows and shops that carry furniture, foliage, or styling supplies you like. Keep your Portable Style File in your bag, car, or carryall along with a tape measure and pen. Now you're ready to hit the road styling!

ideas right at your fingertips...

Part II:
Creating Everyday Indoor Style

At Ease:
Styling the Living Room

4

5

**Good Company:
Styling the Dining
Room and Kitchen**

6

**Sweet Retreats:
Styling the Bedroom
and Bathroom**

Chapter

At Ease: Styling the Living Room

4

Warming Up the Heart of the Home

When I moved at age nineteen from my family home in Washington, D.C., to New York City to become a model with the Ford Modeling Agency, it seemed as if I'd be starting from scratch in everything from my living space to my career. Faced with an empty apartment and a lot more questions than answers about my chosen path, I didn't know where to start. I was excited but paralyzed.

Then my mother reminded me that the only time you start from scratch is when you're born. From there on out, you're working with things you've got.

"Do you want to take your bedroom set?" she asked, ever practical and can-do. Nah. To me, that furniture was precious but passé, a symbol of my childhood. I couldn't show up in the Big Apple with little-girl stuff. Besides, I'd be sharing my bedroom with one of my roommates and wouldn't have room for my canopied double bed and three-tiered purple curtains. What we really needed was a look for the living room, where we'd be entertaining our exciting new friends and becoming part of the trend-setting crowd—or so we hoped! The bedroom set was out, but what Mom said echoed in my head until, as so often in our relationship, I saw the way to my own solution: to look at my resources and put the word out.

My high school boyfriend was also moving away from D.C., but his destination was the beach. I should have realizeid that with me yearning for the big city and his life plan revolving around a beach resort, it wasn't going to work out between us, but that was beside the point. He had a living room set he was willing to sell for a good price. Okay, so it was bright orange, but I bought his living room pieces and headed north, feeling very adult with my first home-furnishing purchase under my belt.

Accordingly, when I arrived in Manhattan, I faced my first adult home styling challenge: To take an orange sofa, orange rug, and other equally arresting bachelor-pad furniture and put together a fashionable, feminine apartment for me and my roommates, who were also models. All that stood between us and a cool bachelorette pad, I assured the girls, was our own creativity.

colors, we were able to make the room come to life—and boy, did we do a lot of living there!

The living room is a logical and lovely place to start styling your life. So much takes place in this central, showpiece space: family gatherings, celebrations, holidays, social events from intimate to grand. Even love often ignites in the living room. Bringing creative energy to this area can quickly change the look of your entire home—and then you can have a party to share your newfound style.

Living rooms have had many looks through the ages. The Victorian parlor often featured an uncomfortable horsehair sofa, perhaps so courting couples didn't get too relaxed. In the sixties, vinyl beanbag chairs often filled trendy conversation pits. The 1980s brought industrial chic, a look that softened in the nineties with fabrics and the perfect solution for

before+after

With orange as the overarching scheme, we had a limited selection of coordinating colors: yellow, lime green, maybe black. I know it sounds gaudy, but it was actually quite bright and cheery. You do what you gotta do—so I added a green pillow to the sofa and my roommate anted up another one in black. I found a yellow lampshade at a thrift store, and picked up a few other items in the same color family simply by keeping my eye out while wandering the streets of the big city. We found a large yellow bowl that we would fill with fruit, mostly oranges, and place on the coffee table. Oranges reminded me of home. Every night Dad would peel one and go around the house offering pieces to me and my brothers; they were good for us, he said. It turned into a family ritual, and since I was incredibly homesick in New York, the orange bowl helped to keep me cheerful, and probably healthy, too. Anyway, by the time we were done, working with what we had and concentrating on a few basic

busy two-career families: slipcovers that came off for easy cleaning.

As different as each of these styles were, they had the common trait of serving the needs of the time, as should your living room. And yet the living room has a real tendency to get stuck and stale. Usually representing a substantial investment in furniture, window and floor coverings, and perhaps artwork, it can become, in effect, a closet filled with dull or outdated clothes too good to get rid of but no fun to wear. Is this room ironically the least alive space in your house? Resurrect it with everyday styling.

In this chapter, I show you three different living room makeovers that make it easy to redo without refinancing. Just by rearranging and bringing in a few different pieces of furniture or spotlighting the right styling supplies, you can give your living or family area a whole new feel—and living for today will become a way of life.

before+after

before+after

before+after

updating with stylish ease

Everybody likes to feel up-to-date, but with fashions changing daily, who can keep up? *You* can—when you're an everyday stylist. You don't have to buy a whole new living room set to take advantage of a trend or to refresh your living room. Updating can be as simple as changing one or two pieces of furniture and pulling a fresh color palette through the room. With the living room's tendency to become more a museum of past tastes than a reflection of the way you live today, thinking "thoroughly modern" can keep your space fresh and fashionable.

Coffee-Table Modern

A high-impact place to start your living room update is with the coffee table, which is often key to the statement of the room and provides a surface perfect for further styling. In this makeover, I went modern with a black iron coffee table topped in Plexiglas. This sleek piece sets the tone for the next moves: a streamlined mid-century wood chair and candles in geometric shapes to light up the new look. The thoroughly modern color palette? Lime green, aluminum, and gray.

Styling Tips

1 **The Simplified Sofa:** Less is more . . . modern, so update your look by limiting the number of items in any space. Here I use just three pillows, one large and two small, all in the same color tone but with the large one a shade darker to add dimension. Simplicity is key to modern design and makes a bolder statement.

2 **Floor-Based Vase:** For a new perspective on a tall vase, move it off the table and onto the floor. Instead of delicate flowers, make a bold statement with tall greens, stalks, and reeds in a similar color palette.

3 **Simple Florals:** For modern simplicity, choose a single variety of flowers, picking up the main color in the room, and arrange

them loosely in a vase.

4 **Geometric Accents:** Geometric shapes are another key to a more organized and modern look, and here they show up in the

form of a spherical vase, a round vase, and square candles in different heights. When scouting the house or stores for styling items,

look for simple geometric shapes in a similar or blending color palette.

singular charm:
styling with a special piece

ave you ever inherited a piece of furniture that you loved, or seen a chair, pillow, or lamp that spoke to you—perhaps from a different era—but didn't tell you how to make it work in your living room? Don't think of such a find as the odd man out. Instead, try using an unusual piece as the springboard to style the living room, taking its characteristics as cues for your color palette and the overall feel. You'll never need to worry about a cookie cutter look when you let that special piece speak for itself.

Vintage Romance and Roses

Who could resist an elegant vintage chair in the shade of deep red roses? Not me, no matter what the current look of my living room. This makeover started with a one-of-a-kind Victorian chair I spotted at a garage sale. Its red velvet upholstery formed the basis of the color palette, which I pulled through to the sofa. See how one special piece can reveal a whole new room?

Since the sofa is often the dominant piece of furniture in your living room, it tends to determine the overall style of the room. If you feel caught on the horns of a dilemma—being stuck with the look or outlaying major cash for a new one—take heart. You can push that beached whale back out into the open water of style.

Everyday Styling Problem: Careworn Sofa

You're bored with your sofa's color or pattern, or lack of one, or it's stained or worn. Maybe you want to change the whole color palette of the room but your sofa seems to limit your styling options.

Everyday Styling Solution: Camouflage

Free yourself by tossing on a solid or print throw. Now you can add pillows to pick up the original tones of the sofa or blend with the throw's color as you like.

Styling Tips

1 **Two-Tone Color Palette:** It takes two to tango, so start any room with a simple two-color palette. Here I've used my red-and-cream theme (shown in chapter 3) and added a third color, green, as an accent with drapes and floral hatboxes.

To find your two-tone palette, start by checking your Style File for color match inspiration. Then grab a pillow, throw, or dish in each color and go around the house looking for matching items. You'll be surprised at what you find. Once your two-tone base is established you can start trying additional colors as accents; it will be easy to see whether or not they work.

2 **Subtler Sofas Have Longer Legs:** When purchasing a new sofa, think neutral so you can restyle at will. I've had these couches for over ten years and in four different houses, and they've looked great in every space. I bring the taupe linen to life with a variety of different pillows as my styling mood changes. You can also give the sofa a new setting by painting an accent color on the wall behind.

3 **Feminine Touches:** To soften the living room's formal atmosphere, try adding feminine touches such as tassels, a skirt on a wing-back chair, a ruffle on a checked pillow, or a fresh bouquet of roses.

4 **Fireplace Foliage:** Bring the outdoors in with a mantel-top topiary garden. Variegated ivy creates a delightfully chaotic contrast to the carefully shaped topiaries, and makes the room come alive—literally.

global warming: bringing the world's colors home

The living room is a wonderful place to go global. In the age of the so-called global village, an international style can simultaneously reflect sophistication and simplicity, individuality and world consciousness. Whether you've inherited family treasures, gathered goodies in your travels, or shop a nearby ethnic market, pieces that represent the rich cultures of the world can add universal appeal and a unique sense of style to your living space. With apologies to the ozone, it's the *good* kind of global warming.

You don't have to limit yourself to one culture or country when bringing the world to your home. I've seen Guatemalan fabrics, Korean pottery, and African woodcarvings displayed together with terrific results.

My mother was of East Indian descent and wore traditional dress, a sari. An eighteen-foot length of cotton or silk that wraps and ties to become a one-piece sheath, a sari is saturated with radiant color—reds and oranges, pinks and blues. Of my mother's many beautiful saris, the one I most liked to see her in was turquoise with hot pink trim and gold embroidery. She wore it when she and my dad went out for special occasions.

It was my job to iron Mom's saris, and I spent so many hours doing it that I remember all the colors and textures in detail. Today, that vision inspires many of my styling decisions. It's interesting how the simplest experiences of childhood, even humdrum chores, can settle deep in our subconscious and then surface in our current sensibilities.

Sari-Inspired Living Room

Because of my ethnic heritage and personal history, in my home I prefer an eclectic mix that includes finds from my travels and family artifacts. I love the vibrant and earthy colors often found in native arts, and I collect such items wherever I am. I store the multicultural styling supplies I'm not using in a trunk, and when I open it up to restyle it's like a treasure chest of international inspiration.

My mother's saris provided the color palette and concept for this living room. Next, I dug into my treasure chest of supplies and found candlesticks and cache boxes, hand-woven textiles and appliqué pieces. What are the threads in your family tapestry? Seek out items that inspire you, whether from your roots or someone else's. The living room is a wonderful place to tell your story, or express your global vision.

Styling Tips

1 **Fabricated Pillows and Throws:** Exotic fabrics from around the world can be used to make inexpensive pillows, drapes, and throws that highlight your theme and add textural dimension to the space. I chose sari silks in strong, contrasting colors for my pillows and throws. Mixing colors creates a sense of abundance and diversity, which underscores the global message.

2 **Pillows with Punch:** Strong colors in the pillows add warmth and vibrance.

3 **Global Village Candle Display:** Light up your spirit as well as your mantel alcove by creating a display of candles in different shapes and sizes. Start with one large candle that goes with your color palette and perhaps echoes your theme. Add smaller candles in different heights to suggest the skyline of a small village.

4 **Hidden Treasures:** Bring out your treasure trove of collections and use them to style a statement about your life in the living room. In this case, mine were cherished items from my family's East Indian heritage and from my own travels.

Chapter

Good Company: Styling the Dining Room and Kitchen

5

feed body and soul...

Setting the Tone to Bring People Together

One Saturday evening a while ago, my husband, Bobby, and I went to two parties. The first was a cocktail party. The house looked ready for an *Architectural Digest* shoot, drinks were top of the line, the food elaborately catered and delicious, the gowns and suits designer, the jewelry aglitter. In attendance were enough Oscar, Grammy, and Emmy winners to have filled out the cast of a Cecil B. DeMille epic. The conversation sparkled with recent deals, mergers, signings, and divorces. We were all at our most elegant and witty. Afterward, Bobby and I went to dinner at Donna's.

Donna and I became great friends years ago, when we were both single and juggling dual careers. Often, at the end of the day, I'd pick up some chicken or fish and head for Donna's house. We'd grill, make a pasta side dish, and put together a salad—Caesar was our favorite and Donna made a great dressing. While she cooked I would style the table—the dining room or the kitchen, depending on our mood—rummaging through her eclectic collection of objets d'art. I would often uncover something hidden away and end up restyling the coffee table or mantel around the special find. She got a kick out of seeing her favorite things displayed in fresh ways, and I loved her collections as much as her cooking.

While we ate, we'd talk about our dreams.

These days, I miss those intimate conversations and impromptu dinners, but that Saturday, as Bobby and I walked in, I realized that although both Donna's life and mine are now fulfilled in new ways—with husbands and children and career success—we still enjoy the same routine.

As usual, there was little time for reflection. I hustled off to the kitchen, where Donna and four other friends were chopping vegetables, mixing salad dressing, and sharing stories about schools and kids.

In the corner of her kitchen she has a small table set up where she juggles the busy schedules of her three young sons. The wall above, filled with calendars, invitations, and artwork tells a rich story of her family's life, and it sets a friendly tone for everyone who walks in the room.

In fact, Donna's entire home is set up in a way that reflects her family's spirit and invites others to join in on everything from stirring the risotto to cutting fresh flowers from the garden. The dining room is always aglow with candles, and the conversation and laughter flow. The kitchen is so cozy you find yourself volunteering for dish detail just to savor one last cup of tea. You usually come away from a night at Donna's with a recipe or two, perhaps a new book to read, and a warm, happy feeling.

Which party do you suppose Bobby and I enjoyed more?

artifacts—grouping them with your silver candlesticks or crystal salt and pepper shakers. Select napkins in a color that picks up, say, the pink in the shells. Let your flowers or centerpiece take off from there, and your table has gone from predictable to an expression of your personal flair.

If instead the occasion is a buffet tasting of Provençal wines and hors d'oeuvres, leave the china in the cupboard and scour the house for pottery and accents in lemon yellow and dusty blue. Replace the candelabra with a pot of fragrant lavender. Suddenly, your bedroom throw becomes a tablecloth, and the party is transported to the south of France.

Just as the dining room can wear many guises, the kitchen is much more than just a place to cook. I'm an avid cook myself, but I find that I still spend many more hours in the kitchen doing all sorts of other things— getting the kids organized, chatting with my husband, talking on the phone, and, of course, eating the quick casual meals that keep us all going through busy days. The kitchen is the main gathering spot of the home—a sort of study, communications center, and café rolled into one. Whether you fill

The ingredients of entertaining are

Style Feeds Body and Soul

The dining room and kitchen are where energy is renewed, where you nourish people with food, the beauty of the space, and the warmth of your bond. When you entertain, you want your style to shine in a way that lets your guests know how glad you are they came. Casual suppers with family or friends may be simpler but should still feel special, festive, uniquely yours. You can accomplish all of this when you serve up style alongside every meal, and feed the soul with extra attention to the personal details.

Everyday styling can make cooking, eating, and entertaining a heartfelt celebration. Think of this space as a living thing, evolving with the occasion, the season, and the mood you want to share. In the dining room, for instance, forget the room's formal reputation and make it suit the moment. You don't have to own a full set of fine china, crystal, or real silver to set the table for a sit-down dinner, and if you do, there's no need to stare at the same old assembly of wedding gifts. This time, style the table by gathering items from a personal collection—ceramic birds, shells,

it with precision cookware worthy of a professional chef or just need to make sure you've got clear passage to the microwave, you want your kitchen to offer a warm welcome to all comers.

Are there messages posted on the refrigerator of your kitchen, report cards and art projects taped to cabinets, school books stashed in a corner? Any of these are sign #1 that your kitchen has importance beyond slicing, dicing, and getting the dishes done.

When you have friends in for dinner, are you as likely to pull chairs up to the kitchen table as to eat in the dining room? Sign #2: Your kitchen possesses multiple identities and a powerful draw.

At a party, do you always find a group hanging out in the kitchen, leaning on the counters and talking away, no matter how hard you might entreat them to come sit in the living room like civilized people? Sign #3: Your kitchen has a life of its own.

Food brings us together in the timeless quest for company, nourishment, and pleasure. When you style your kitchen and dining room to sustain the soul, every day is an opportunity to savor the taste of the good life.

there to promote friendship and fun.

special occasions:
styling the sit-down dinner table

When the occasion is special, you want to "dress" the dining room just as you would dress yourself for a big night. With this in mind I usually draw upon a favorite fashion concept to create spectacular sit-down tables. Back in my early modeling days I was introduced to the tone-on-tone color palette by a top model wearing an array of whites and creams, from her knit cap to her sleek leather boots. I immediately fell in love with this mix of textures and tones. But I don't limit myself to a single tone. Often, my outfit is composed of several different shades of cream or ivory, not because I'm color-blind but because the difference is what makes it interesting. At the same time, the look is very appealing to the eye because all the shades blend. This effect is what the fashion industry calls "tone-on-tone," and the concept can make an elegant statement in your dining room as well.

Tone-on-Tone Table

One of the best ways to style a special-occasion table without investing in a lot of formal dinnerware is to use mismatched objects in the same color family but with different shades and hues, yielding a tone-on-tone result rich in visual appeal and often easy on the pocketbook. On this formal table, shades of white and cream against one another add dimension. Match them perfectly and the look goes flat. Layered tablecloths, eclectic but elegant tableware, and accents such as strategically grouped candles and delicate floral stems complete the tone-on-tone template. Style your table so there's an interplay between unity and contrast and you'll see how easy special occasions can be.

forked place cards

Placement is everything. Don't think of place cards as just a frivolous little addition to your formal table. If the right placement of guests can fire up lively conversation, then place cards are your spark. Hit the stationery or art store for card stock in your color scheme and a calligraphy pen; if you like, you can trim the edges of the cards with pinking shears. A vintage fork on a plate makes a unique place card holder.

from your style file:

Find Your Tone-on-Tone Palette

To identify likely candidates for your tone-on-tone table palette, go to the Dining Room section of your Style File and look for the colors that appeal to you most. Do you tend toward traditional ivory, or soft earth browns? Perhaps you're yearning for an urban contemporary look in shades of black, gray, and silver. Take paint samples or fabric swatches in the colors you're attracted to and play around with your tear sheets to find the palette that you like best.

Note that certain colors work better than others. Neutrals make great candidates for tone-on-tone effects—creams, whites, and ivories; beige, khaki, and brown; various shades of silver and gray. Brighter colors such as reds, blues, and greens need to share a basic hue in order to artfully blend. Be sure to give combinations from these color families a careful eye to avoid visual chaos.

painter's-cloth underskirt

A large tablecloth that falls all the way to the floor can add a look of sumptuous luxury to your dining room, but cloths of this size can be hard to find. End your search at the paint store or hardware store, where you can buy a painter's cloth big enough to cover your table's top and legs (remember to measure before you go as they come in a variety of sizes). Use the painter's cloth as the first of several layers, adding tablecloths in tone-on-tone shades at alternating angles. A quilted bed coverlet can be used as an unexpected alternative to the painter's cloth base.

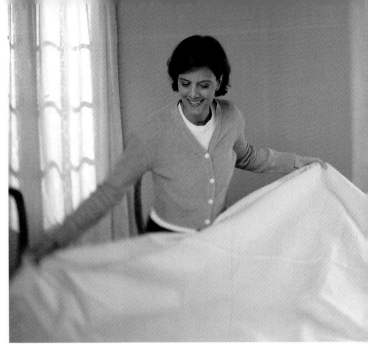

Styling Tips

1 **Elegant Old Silver:** Silver adds formality and a sense of history to any dining table, but you don't need a perfectly matched, freshly polished service to set a stunning table. Achieve an Old World elegance by collecting mismatched heirloom silver from swap meets and estate sales—vases, trays, tea pots, and the like. When it's time for a special dinner, bring it all to the table without polishing it, to emphasize its vintage feel.

2 **Mixing Plates, Matching Chargers:** Add a subtle variation to your dishware, too, by collecting china in several different patterns that have tones of common colors. Then, set the formal table with a silver charger (an oversize service plate) under each of your assorted plates. Your eyes will feast on the ever-changing plate patterns while the coordinated chargers pull it all together.

3 **Candle Bouquets:** I like to arrange candles like flowers, grouping them together in a beautiful bouquet of light. To bring radiance to your table, gather candles of different heights but in the same tone-on-tone color palette. Place several on a plate, interspersing taller candles with smaller ones so the individual points of light stand out.

4 **All-White Florals:** Though you may think first of using flowers to *add* color to a space, when you're styling tone-on-tone, new colors can distract from your subtly layered palette, so see what happens when you bring only white blossoms to the table. I like to use a variety of species, such as mums, white lilies, lisianthus, dianthus, baby's breath, stock, and dahlia, selecting just a few of each and placing them in individual vases scattered around the table.

a recipe to suit the occasion

This table was styled for a "progressive" dinner party. That meant everyone contributed a portion of the meal, but also that the party traveled to a new home for every course. The evening turned into a wonderful collage of individual sensibilities and styles, pulsing with the energy of self-expression.

My assignment was dessert. I wanted to make something that was light and lovely to look at that could be prepared ahead of time. I settled on poached pears floating on crème anglaise, decorated with hearts drawn with apricot preserves. I served them with a dessert wine, followed by tea, coffee, and cookies. I felt the pears had a lovely elegance, and worked perfectly with the tone-on-tone table.

dress your dining room *and* yourself

You've worked hard to dress up your dining room for an elegant evening's entertainment. Now, dress yourself to enhance rather than clash with the look.

Consider the tone, mood, and color palette you've already established, and when you find yourself standing in front of the closet moments before your guests are due to arrive, the "what am I going to *wear?*" routine is easily resolved.

Poached Pears with Apricot Glaze Hearts

Poached pears:

6–8 Bosc pears

2 cups water

Pinch of salt

3–4 cinnamon sticks

4 whole cloves

1 cup sugar

1 cup apricot preserves

Crème anglaise:

1 cup milk

4 egg yolks, slightly beaten

$1/4$ cup sugar

Pinch of salt

$1/2$ vanilla bean pod, cut into three pieces

(or 1 teaspoon vanilla extract)

2–3 tablespoons Grand Marnier liqueur (optional)

• Select pears that are firm with no soft spots. Carefully peel the whole pears with a stainless steel knife to avoid discoloration, leaving the stems in place. Do not core. Place the water, salt, cinnamon sticks, and cloves into a nonreactive pan and place over medium heat. Bring to a boil. Using a long-handled spoon, gently place the pears in the boiling mixture and reduce the heat at once. Add sugar and simmer on low until the pears are tender, remove from heat, and allow to cool. Drain the syrup and carefully remove the pears. Do not pick them up by their stems or the stems may come off.

• Heat the apricot preserves in a pan for 5 to 7 minutes, allowing the mixture to bubble a bit as it thickens and darkens slightly. Remove from heat, cool for a few minutes, and strain. Transfer the strained sauce into a squeeze applicator bottle (like the kind used for hair color).

• To make the crème anglaise, scald the milk in a double boiler, then slowly stir in the egg yolks, sugar, salt, and vanilla bean (if you use vanilla extract, wait and stir it into the cooled custard later). Continue to stir constantly until the mixture thickens, then remove from heat and continue to stir the custard as it cools to release the steam. If you are using vanilla extract or liqueur, add it now. Cover and chill. This can be made up to 24 hours ahead of time.

• To serve, cover the bottom of each plate with crème anglaise and carefully place a pear on top. For each heart, squeeze two drops of the apricot glaze side by side onto the crème anglaise. Drag a thin wooden skewer through each dot to draw each side of the heart shape. Continue until you have as many hearts as you want. *Serves 6–8*

In an earlier part of my life I was the co-owner of a restaurant on Melrose Avenue in Los Angeles. Exciting and glamorous, yes, but guess what? Suddenly I was entertaining nightly whether I felt like it or not, and sometimes for hundreds of people at a time! Much as I love to throw dinner parties, this was a whole new ballgame.

It's one thing when someone is coming to your home; let's face it, how mad can anybody be about a free meal? But in the restaurant business, with paying customers, you'd better believe it's another story. The table settings, the food, the servers, décor, presentation, and

appetite for life:
styling an easy buffet

flowers—I discovered that everything had to be just right or our guests wouldn't return.

In addition to playing the gracious host, one of my nightly tasks at Bono's was to make sure that the antipasto bar, the tables, and the bar were styled. It was quite a challenge to make the buffet different and appealing every night. I used breads, fabrics, napkins, herbs, pottery, flowers, candles, and vases—whatever came to hand or mind. I was always turning over a dish to get height or using an odd container for display. I had to be creative, usually all in just twenty minutes or so before the dinner rush.

A well-styled buffet table can turn what is a serving convenience into a striking visual spectacle. There's more to it than just putting the food on the table in your best serving dishes. Contrast is a buffet's best friend, and you can find it in the different heights, sizes, and colors of the foods, dishes, and accessories.

Style-to: Flower Petal Napkin Fold

Flat is the enemy on a buffet table, so don't just let your napkins lie there. This folding technique turns napkins into 3-D flowers, and once you catch on, it's a snap. Even your kids will have fun helping out.

• Use napkins in two contrasting colors.
• Lay your first napkin out on the table, top side down, and fold each corner into the middle.
• Fold each corner in again.
• Place one hand flat under the napkin and the other on top and turn the napkin over. Again fold in each corner.
• Place your fingers flat in the middle to hold the folds as you gently lift each corner and tug on the flap underneath. Repeat the process with all four sides.
• Fold the rest of the napkins the same way, then layer them in alternating colors for a fabulous flower petal effect.

style with food & color

Harmony between food and décor is part of a great party. To make great match-ups, pull appealing recipes from magazines and newspapers and file them in the Dining Room folder of your Style File behind tear sheets that align with the same theme.

The Bountiful Buffet

To buff up your buffet-styling skills, start with your Portable Style File. Write down the dimensions of the table or sideboard you use so that you can keep an eye out for linen sales and assemble a tabletop wardrobe to cover any occasion—formal or informal, summer or winter, brunch or cocktails and snacks.

Next, choose your color scheme based on the tablecloth you plan to use, either by picking colors out of the pattern, or, if you have a solid cloth, by choosing a contrasting color. Select at least two colors.

Now shop your own home for styling items, carrying the tablecloth with you. Gather candlesticks, bowls, baskets, platters, pots, serving spoons—whatever works in terms of color or texture, whether or not it's something you've used in the dining room before. Bring it all along.

Start experimenting with the placement of the serving dishes and styling items you've gathered. Begin by building height in the back, then work your way across the table and forward. Practice serving yourself to see if the arrangement seems to flow as you move along. Adjust accordingly until the table feels just right.

Use the buddy system to make styling your buffet even more fun. Invite a friend to come early and lend a creative eye and hand.

Height adds panache to a buffet display, so to elevate a dish, stack two platters back to back. Roll a piece of duct tape and stick it in between the platters so that the top one doesn't slide off when guests serve themselves.

the everyday kitchen: **styling for casual cheer**

Our son, Hutton, hangs out almost exclusively in the kitchen. He does his homework, plays board games, and does projects, all at the kitchen table. Little Hailey's highchair, with a constantly changing collection of toys (a precocious everyday stylist herself), graces the landscape, too. And it's not unusual to find my husband, Bobby, in the kitchen with an oversize spreadsheet and graphs laid out on the table, plotting the next morning's commodity trades. Why work in the home office when the fridge can be within arm's reach?

When a friend drops by to say hi or for a cup of tea and a chat, we sit in the kitchen; and yes, my informal entertaining meals are often served just steps from the stove if the weather doesn't invite us outside. What better place to dig into a bowl of hot homemade chicken soup?

Gather fabulous ingredients and mix

from your style file:

Recipe for a Fabulous Kitchen

To come up with your own personal recipe for the style of your kitchen, consider all its uses and pleasures. It's where you create culinary wonders of the world and cozy breakfasts, share secrets over a salad with friends, or simply gaze out the window with a cup of coffee in your hands. Make a list of everything that goes on in your kitchen, and for each activity, come up with one or two styling ideas that could enhance the room's usefulness and beauty—a windowsill herb garden, a classic print on the wall above the table, a new cover for that fuzzy old dog bed. Use your Style File and the tips in this chapter to spark your vision. Now you're ready to cook up some style anytime you're hungry for a change!

and adjust until the result feels right.

Styling Tips

1 **Cabinet Cache:** If you're accustomed to thinking of cabinets as places to hide things away, instead think *display*. As if you were styling a gallery case or shop window, show off anything from French bistro canisters to hand-painted salt and pepper shakers straight from your cabinet shelves. Got more items than space? Keep them on hand to rotate whenever you're ready for a new view.

2 **Glassware with Sass:** Pull your kitchen's color scheme from favorite glassware or dishes that you like to keep on display.

3 **Blackboard Fun:** The kitchen is a communications center, so why not add some style to your notes to others and self? Choose your nook and put a blackboard on the wall. Get a box of colored chalk, then spend a few moments each week dressing it up with original drawings and borders and reminders that are sure to make you smile.

4 **Fresh Linens:** For a warm finishing touch to the kitchen counter, stack up a few fresh dishtowels in colors that pick up your dishware or cabinets. A countertop stash softens the view and keeps a clean towel within easy reach.

kitchen collections: styling unique displays

Putting your collections on display is an everyday styling principle, and I'd bet money that somewhere in your house you have at least the beginning of a collection perfect for bringing a sense of fun and even family history to your kitchen. Are a dozen of your mother's tin cookie cutters hidden away in a bottom drawer? Do you have some pretty copper pans on hand? A half-dozen mismatched teacups? Bring them out and put them on view, playing around with placement until the appliances fade into the background and your personal style takes center stage. If you're a real collector with some unusual salt and pepper shakers, vintage kitchenware, or other special finds, consider making your collection a focal point of the room. If you're not much of a collector now, it's easy to become one. Whenever you see something special that will perfectly set off a treasure you already have, pick it up on the spot.

Styling Tips

1 **Grouping:** Instead of scattering your collections here and there, group them together to make a more powerful statement.

2 **Tea for Two:** A teacup collection adds old-fashioned whimsy and a welcoming touch.

3 **Cookie Cutters:** Display your cookie cutters in a tall glass jar to create a delightful collage of shapes and images.

4 **Transferware Uncovered:** Pull your dish collection out of the cupboard and onto a sideboard for all to admire.

Forget the formal look when
Any nook or cranny will do

curating your kitchen collection...
Surprise is the essence of style

*T*rue, a good cook can improvise many a dish based on ingredients at hand, but for a masterpiece, the individual elements must complement each other. Most great recipes are born from ingredients in the same family of flavors. Pasta, basil, tomatoes, and garlic can be happily combined to create a number of Italian dishes. Pumpernickel bread, cheeses, sliced meats, and pickles are the principal materials for a platter of Danish open-faced sandwiches. A good meal has a theme, and you can use this synergistic scheme to style the space you cook in, too.

flavor of the month:
styling a theme kitchen

Once you've settled on a theme, clear the kitchen space you plan to style. Choose an item that represents the theme and color scheme you want to work with—perhaps a dish, pottery piece, cookbook, or tablecloth—and take it as your bloodhound on a hunt around the house. Pull out everything you have that might relate to the color palette and/or theme, which could include spices, food, dishes and vases, linens, posters or pictures, books, musical instruments, candles, knickknacks and objets d'art, and so on. Group the styling items together on a table and see which ones blend and work together, and which ones stand out like sore thumbs. Put the clunkers away.

Place the largest piece first. Then, moving forward, layer in the additional items. Stand back after every few additions to see how they look. Remember, you don't have to use everything just because you have it.

Change your kitchen's theme whenever it starts to feel tired. Your kitchen will feel as fresh as the food you cook.

Italian Trattoria

Anyone can transform a kitchen into a *trattoria* before you can say "antipasto"! In this rustic kitchen corner I gathered food, utensils, pottery, and herbs inspired by the Tuscan countryside, then placed them to evoke a pasta dinner in the making.

Picchio Pacchio
Tomato-Basil-Garlic Pasta

This was called "Susie's favorite" on the menu at the restaurant. Light, flavorful, and easy to make, the recipe represents the essence of the everyday kitchen because you can whip it up in minutes and yet eat in style.

1/2 pound cappellini (angel hair pasta)
1 teaspoon salt
1/2 cup olive oil
8 cloves fresh garlic, minced or
    pressed
6 large ripe tomatoes, chopped
1 bunch fresh basil leaves, torn
Salt and pepper to taste
Parmesan cheese (optional)

• For the pasta, bring to a boil a large pot of water, adding in a teaspoon of salt.
• In a separate saucepan, heat up the olive oil over medium heat and lightly sauté the garlic (do not brown).
• Add in the tomatoes, mix gently, and cook until soft. Don't over-stir.
• Tear the basil leaves as you add them to the mixture.
• Salt to taste.
• While making the sauce, cook the pasta according to the directions on the box. Do not cover while cooking.
• When done, drain and rinse the pasta under cool water briefly and transfer to a serving dish.
• Add the fresh tomato, basil, garlic mixture on top of the pasta, and toss lightly.
• Grate fresh Parmesan cheese right onto each individual plate as desired.
Serves 4

Note: Do not break the pasta before cooking—it's much more fun to eat it the way the Italians do. Nice long pieces that wind for days around your fork.

from your style file:

Recipe for a Theme

To assemble the ingredients for your themed kitchen, leaf quickly through all the sections of your Style File, looking for tear sheets that bring a certain theme to mind. Are there several pieces of Italian pottery, for example, or a few Asian-inspired rooms with cool, lean lines? Have you cut out lots of pictures of country-style ideas, from barns to daisies to wooden churns? Perhaps you see elements of a '50s diner—chrome and vinyl furniture, primary colors, curving shapes—or the dusty pastels and native artwork of the American Southwest. There's no reason you can't swipe a bedroom or garden theme for your kitchen. Style transcends the earthbound categories of terra firma!

will feel as fresh as the food you cook.

Styling Tips

1 **See-Through Pasta:** Pasta, in all its wonderful shapes, sizes, and colors, looks great in clear glass canisters on the counter. Fill each canister with a different type of pasta and place them next to other bottled condiments in the same color palette as your theme.

2 **Stacked Dishes:** Repeat your color scheme with a casual stack of dishes displayed next to other objects in the same palette.

3 **Styling with Food:** Sure, you can leave your veggies in the fridge and your spices in the cupboard, but why not let them out for all to see, celebrating the room's *raison d'être* and Mother Nature's bounty?

4 **Indoor Herb Garden:** Fresh herbs can wake up any dish, elevating the flavor from humdrum to five-star, but you'll only use them if you have them on hand. Pick up your favorite culinary herbs at the nursery and pot them in assorted containers for a mini chef's garden right in your own kitchen.

Chapter

Sweet Retreats: Styling the Bedroom and Bathroom

6

fresh starts...

Waking Up to Everyday Styling

It was about nine o'clock in the evening and I took a break from writing to go up and tuck Hutton into bed. It was dark as I reached down to kiss him, and I screamed when I got a furry face instead. I snapped on the light to find Kiwi, our Labrador–golden retriever mix, snuggled between the sheets with a down comforter tucked around her and her head on a brand new goose-down pillow.

True, I had agreed when we got Kiwi that she could sleep on Hutton's bed. I had envisioned the close bond between a boy and his dog, probably from watching *Lassie* when I was growing up, but in my vision, the dog slept at the foot of the bed. Now I'm buying goose-down pillows for the pampered mutt?

"Does Kiwi really have to sleep on the new sixty-dollar goose-down pillow?" I asked Hutton.

"I don't mind. G'night, Mom."

As I walked out, I heard snoring.

"Hutton," I whispered. "She snores, too?"

"Yeah, Mom, she snores, but I don't mind. Good night."

It's moments like this that make memories for you and your kids. And what's more important in the scheme of things—a child having the joy of cuddling with his dog, or a crisp clean bed with no dog hairs?

You decide.

Like any space in the house, bedrooms should reflect the style of the people who sleep in them. In the case of my son, that seems to include a certain quota of frogs and snails and puppy dogs' tails. Perhaps you'd like your bedroom—and your cuddling—to be a little less . . . zoo-logical? Each person has unique needs, and it's nice to keep those in mind when styling the space where we awake every day.

What could be more inspiring than to wake up in a space that you've made beautiful with your own personal style?

As the name implies, everyday styling is meant to energize each and every day. Bringing style into your bedroom jump-starts a creative life, revitalizing your attitude with every sunrise and providing a blissful retreat as the day draws to a close. Not only are your bedroom and bath-room places where you spend about a third of your life but also where you rejuvenate your mind, body, and soul. Fill your bed and bath with style to open up your eyes to everyday beauty.

Start styling with a simple question: What is your bedroom to you? The one place you can always relax? Your retreat from the bustle of life? A sanctuary for uninterrupted work or reading? A sweet love nest? All of those things? With your peace of mind and perhaps your love life in the balance, you don't want to look at this space with sleepy eyes. Use style to rejuvenate your private retreat, and to ease your body and soul into each brand new day.

from your style file:

Balancing form and function in the bedroom—the most personal of spaces—can sometimes seem a little tricky. Your Style File can help unstick your styling efforts and lead you to the mix you seek in your retreat.

1. Open the Bedroom section in your Style File binder. If you haven't started working with these tear sheets yet or want additional ideas, grab your original Bedroom folder, too.

2. Take a slip of paper and jot down a few notes about the feeling you want in your bedroom. Restful and quiet? Bright and sunny? Romantic? Sexy? Zen-like and serene?

3. Compare your tear sheets to the feel you're looking for. How do the colors, textures, and arrangements correspond? If you think you're after a meditative effect but all your colors are bold and bright, this conflict could make it difficult to get started styling. Experiment with your Style File as described in chapter 3, pulling more tear sheets if necessary, to home in on the components of your bedroom style. Does a spectacular baroque bedstead suggest you might want to experiment beyond your current modern look? Is it a quality of clear light you love, which you could achieve by swapping your heavy drapes for sheer white curtains? Perhaps you think you like the colors in a picture when the intimacy of the canopy is the actual draw.

4. Once your vision is in place, raid the linen closet, dining room sideboard, and sewing room to gather your styling supplies. Borrow pillows from the living room; snag an afghan from the family room. Dig up blankets, throws, tablecloths, and runners to add the textures and colors you see in your Style File and in your mind.

5. Use your tear sheets and the style-to's and tips in this chapter as starting points, and plunge ahead!

love is in the air:
styling for romance

We can't ignore the fact (and who would want to!) that the bedroom is the center of romantic activity. But just as your favorite ratty old pajamas have a way of killing the mood, so can those computer manuals piled up on the nightstand, a laundry basket left on the dresser, or an electronic arcade complete with TV, computer, and the full complement of 21st-century gadgets. What mere libido could hope to compete?

Call me a romantic, but I believe that sensual bedroom styling deserves more attention than lighting a few candles from time to time. Setting the mood is the essence of sharing. Style provides the method.

Start with the practical. If you're partnered, it's time for some honest conversation about styling the bedroom so that it works for both of you, meeting mutual wants and needs. If your mate hates lace and ruffles or purple and pink or slippery satin sheets, these wouldn't make top picks for promoting romantic harmony. However, if the prospect of sneaking into your boudoir turns him on, feminine or sexy is just fine. Consider logistics, too. If one of you likes to sit up reading when the other is early-to-bed, an easy chair with a reading light in the master suite can let you be together while following your individual rhythms. Don't forget a place for a CD player and that mood music you both love.

Styling together is an intimate journey, so try not to interrogate your partner or ask for decisions out of thin air. Share your Style File pictures from the Bedroom and Bathroom section. Add in some pictures that you think might appeal to your partner's taste. Take some time for window-shopping together in the linen section of department stores and see what kinds of colors and textures you both like. You may make some interesting discoveries!

Once you've established common ground, go to town with the sensual touches that can keep your romance fresh, day and night.

Boudoir Bed

The magic of love lies in a sense of shared intimacy, and you can easily turn your bed into a private island for any special romantic occasion with a few simple touches. Whether it be a canopy drape or a special card on the pillow, it's the thought that warms the heart; the effort that affirms the affinity between you and your partner.

Style-to: Romantic Canopy

You don't have to have a frilly bedroom to take advantage of a romantic canopy. A simple, inexpensive swoop of white netting can create a romantic effect that's easy to put up for special nights without committing to it for every day. Pick up a ready-made canopy as I did here, or make your own in a flash.

Styling supplies:

Cup hook

Large drapery ring

10 feet of tuille or netting

- Screw the cup hook into the ceiling, centered above the bed.
- Hook the ring onto the cup hook.
- Pull the fabric through the ring to the midpoint, draping it over the bed and tucking it behind the headboard.

Decorative pillows can be pricey, so if you're doing your bed on a budget, use regular bed pillows and cover them in attractive shams in the same color. For extra panache add just one large European square pillow and perhaps a small bolster to soften the lines. The uniform color and varied pillow shapes can create a very upscale look at a reasonable price.

rose nosegay

Roses cut straight from the garden often have short or odd length stems. Take advantage of nature's eclectic sensibility by grouping roses that don't make the long-stem grade tightly together in a teapot, short vase, or small pitcher, creating a beautiful nosegay.

Styling Tips

1 **Lovable Breakfast Tray:** Set the mood early in the day with a little lingering in bed . . . and some breakfast to fuel the fire. Find a charming breakfast tray—I like this wicker tray with handles and sides for easy handling in bed—and line it with a nice linen. If you like going to flea markets you can pick up a few vintage teacups and saucers that don't match (the less they match the more style they add). Final touch: a fresh cut flower from the garden.

2 **Fabric Bedcover Camouflage:** Transform your bed with a single piece of fabric and *voilà*: a quick bedcover makeover. At the fabric store, pick a pattern or solid in the color palette you've chosen. Have it cut a bit longer on each side than the width of your mattress. Lay it over a sheet or down comforter to create what looks like the top of a duvet or a coverlet. Use this technique with any fabric you like for a fast bedroom wardrobe change.

3 **Rose-Petal Bed:** A scattering of flower petals, a book of poetry, a breakfast tray, and thou . . . For a romantic surprise that's easy to do any day of the year, ask the florist for a half dozen day-old roses. Gently pull off the heads and sprinkle the petals on the bed. *Tip:* This looks best on white linens.

Blueberry Cream Cheese Breakfast-in-Bed Muffins

Hutton's teacher, Joan, created this incredible secret muffin recipe, seeking good body and brain fuel for the kids who come to school without breakfast. I told Joan I just had to have her recipe for my book because it was such a great low-sugar, high-energy muffin—but she said it was a secret. Hmm . . .

"Don't worry," I said. "Your secret is safe with me—and every single one of my readers."

1 heaping cup whole wheat flour

1 heaping cup all-purpose flour (you can substitute high-protein bread flour)

1 heaping cup uncooked old-fashioned rolled oats

3/4 cup granulated sugar

1/2 cup powdered nonfat milk

1 tablespoon baking powder

1/2 teaspoon salt

2 large eggs, beaten

3/4 cup unsweetened applesauce

1 cup water, room temperature

3/4 cup frozen blueberries

4 ounces cream cheese

Butter for top

• Preheat the oven to 350°. Grease a 12-cup muffin tin.

• Mix the dry ingredients in a large bowl. Make a well in the center of the mixture and pour in the eggs, applesauce, and water. Mix gently until thoroughly combined.

• Stir in the blueberries.

• Take half an 8-ounce package of cream cheese. Cut it in half, then cut each half into 6 equal slices. Spoon 1 heaping tablespoon of batter into each muffin cup. Place a pat of cream cheese on top of the batter, then fill the cups with the remaining batter all the way to the top.

• Bake 20–25 minutes or until golden brown. Do not undercook. Remove from oven and top with a little butter. *Yields 12 muffins*

Go to town with the sensual touches

Styling Tips

1 **Scented Sachet:** What is fragrance but beauty unseen? Waft a lovely scent over your intimate moments with a small sachet

tied with a pretty ribbon hung from a knob on a cabinet door. Every swing of the door will reawaken your most primal sense.

2 **Glow of Romance:** Soft light is just right for setting a romantic mood. Try a bedside oil lamp for a warm glow with the

flattering color tones of flame. Use caution to prevent fires of the type you didn't mean to start!

that can keep your romance fresh.

3 **Love Letters:** You don't have to be a poet to deploy the potent arrow of words in Cupid's quiver. Find a book of beautiful love poems or letters and have it on hand to read passages aloud to each other—or quietly to yourself.

4 **Rose Topiary:** Long stemmed roses are lovely loose in a tall vase—but why not refresh your romantic landscape by tying them up in a topiary ball instead? Pull them together, tie tightly at the base of the blooms, then place the stems in a vase or a decorative container filled with floral foam. Add variegated ivy and ferns and finish with a cascade of ribbon.

three pieces do it

When you want to quickly furnish a bedroom without getting caught in cookie cutter drab, just think three from the flea market: a side table, end table, and chair. Don't worry if your finds don't match. A fresh coat of paint will tie it all together to create a whole new space on a budget your accountant will readily approve.

head to toe:
dressing your bed

*T*he main act in the bedroom is—surprise!—the bed. The largest piece of furniture and the most important, the bed also happens to *love* being styled. Its sweeping expanse awaits your linens and accessories, all of which you can swap at the drop of a hat with your mood, the seasons, or simply because today is different than yesterday.

Begin by rearranging the room, if you can, so that the bed is center stage as you come through the door. Now consider how you use your bed, and don't stop at the obvious zzz's. Do you, like the famous French author Colette, read and write reclined *au lit?* If so, stock the area with pillows that offer back support, a writing surface (you can get handsome laptop desks in a variety of designs), a place to stack books and magazines within easy reach, and a good reading light. Do you enjoy afternoon naps or quiet periods of meditation? An afghan or throw draped at the foot can keep you covered and cozy, and you won't have to remake the bed after a brief rest. If you're styling a guest room that will also see service as a den, scout around for a daybed that doubles as a sofa.

Now, go crazy dressing up your bed from head to toe. Linens, coverlets, quilts, duvets; blankets and bedspreads; pillows in a thousand shapes, sizes, and patterns; and an assortment of accessories, small touches, and unexpected imports from other parts of the house are all available to make your bed's fashion statement and sweeten your personal retreat.

Country Cabin to Elegant Antique Bedroom

When I saw this room, with its exposed beams and all-wood walls and floors, it screamed rustic cabin—the perfect opportunity to introduce a strong, bright red and indulge in a delicious mix of patterns. The result was pure country charm.

Then, taking my inspiration from a small vintage lamp, I switched tracks to style the same bed for refined antique elegance. With soft textures to play against the rough-hewn walls, the room now had a more feminine touch.

A new look in the bedroom revitalizes

Styling Tips

1 **Linen Latitudes:** Whether you mix prints for maximum personality or layer a few different shades of the same hue to dress

the bed in "tone-on-tone," linens expand your bedroom's horizons. Use them to traverse the whole world of style.

2 **Bedroom Blooms:** Don't forget flowers for the bedroom! Use your bedding colors as the basis for selecting fresh blooms

to brighten the side table, or try three small vases and three kinds of flowers in similar shades. Perfume your dreams to bring them

to blossom.

3 **Sitting Pretty:** A chair by the bed offers a transition between being up and about and stretching out to sleep. For an aged look,

paint or stencil the backrest, then when dry lightly sand certain spots down to the wood. Some fresh fruit or a carafe of water adds a

welcoming bedside touch for your guests.

think outside the box: styling the bathroom

In the home we recently bought, the areas that needed the most remodeling were the master bedroom and bathroom. I had to take out a vintage tile bathroom, which just killed me, but we needed space for a closet and shower. I toyed with the idea of putting in another vintage bathroom until, while browsing through my Style File, I noticed that the photos I'd collected had a warmer look than the hard tile did, and showed spaces that were more like an extension of the bedroom. I remembered, too, that I love carpet in the bathroom to provide a soft landing for bare feet (throw rugs near the shower keep the carpet dry). So, based on my Style File, I built my sanctuary on the colors and tones of the bedroom, even bringing in the same carpet to join the two spaces and make the entire master suite seem bigger. And, beautiful as that old tile bathroom was, I don't miss it. This one is relaxing, renewing, and thoroughly Susie-style.

As in the bedroom, the well-styled bathroom unites form and function to serve your family's needs and please all your senses during your daily routines. In fact, with its soft carpet and layered rugs, our bathroom is so cozy that the kids and dog are always hanging out there while Bobby and I get ready for work. It's one of the nicest morning family-time places in the house—but come evening, my bathroom becomes my private retreat, where I soak in a warm tub and reflect on my day. From morning's energy to evening's meditation, the well-styled bathroom rejuvenates the body and soul. All you need to do is think outside the bathroom's box and indulge yourself in everyday style.

The Everyday Spa

You are the driving force for all that happens in your life—so don't you deserve a little time out? A beautiful bathroom complete with a hot, fragrant tub flanked by candlelight, exquisite flowers, and all the supplies you need for self-pampering—you can style a mini-spa right into your everyday bathroom.

I love my evening bath and sometimes stay in it for hours, mixing in bubbles, bath salts, or oils according to my mood and adding hot water as needed. I find it prime creative time. While I cleanse my mind, soothe my soul, and beautify my skin, I'm also likely to pore through magazines and pull out tear sheets, tossing them from the bath one by one.

toiletry tea tray

You know all those bottles full of magic elixirs designed to make you look and feel your best? Many of them are pretty good-looking themselves, thanks to the cosmetic industry's dedication to packaging. Rather than crowd your shelves and drawers, leverage your toiletry investment by putting the treasures on display. Find a silver or mirrored tray and select old perfume bottles, silver items, or body splashes from your collection. Create a graceful arrangement and display your vanity tray on the bathroom counter.

Styling Tips

1 **Two-Tone Accessories:** Harmony is key to an everyday spa, and I like to achieve it by choosing two colors with which to style the bathroom. Here it was classic white and soft green, based on candles and bath salts I'd received as gifts. Choose two colors that spell "spa" to you and draw them through your bathroom. When it's time for a new look, choose two new colors and begin again.

2 **Custom Vintage Linens:** Dress up your vanity with collected or inherited hand towels, which you can customize by adding vintage buttons or lace trim.

3 **Bath Salts:** Instead of keeping bath salts in their container, pour them into a nice dish and keep it by your bath. Now they're as visually appealing as they are practical.

4 **Orchid in a Bottle:** An orchid's bloom suspended in bath oil is a delicate work of art. Keep a look out for those special spa items that can enhance your personal retreat.

candles to radiate and reflect

Who says fire and water don't mix? Lighting candles sets the mood for a lovely long soak in the tub, so turn the soap holder into a meditation niche by filling it with small votive candles in your color palette. You might also use the tub's edge or a ledge that's large enough to be safe.

Mirrors make a great backdrop for candles anywhere in the house, and the bathroom is no exception. Try a simple grouping of candles in colors similar to the mirror's trim to frame the bathroom mirror when unlit; light them up and see their radiance reflected throughout the room. When you're entertaining, lit candles are an especially nice touch in a guest bathroom.

5 **Mirror, Mirror, on the Wall:** Even the sink can be simply styled for added interest.

Leaning paintings and mirrors against a wall instead of hanging them adds an element of surprise and an attractively different line to the room—both welcome amid the hard surfaces and predictable form of many bathrooms. You can add loads of character to your space with an interesting mirror and this leaning technique; no hammer or nails required. I put this gilded beauty from the flea market here to see if I liked it, and it seems right—so for the moment I'm leaving it just the way it is.

Infuse your simplest routines with everyday style. Take a moment to reap the rewards you deserve. See how no two days are alike and beauty surrounds you in ever changing ways.

Style-to:
Orchid Arrangement

I love orchids—and though they can be expensive, the blooms can also last up to three months if you care for them correctly. Orchids love the steam and indirect light in the bathroom. You don't have to water them more than once every seven to ten days, when you can just put them in the tub, run the water over them, let the water drain through the soil, and then put them back in their spot.

Styling supplies:

Planting container

Orchid potting soil

1–3 orchid plants

Curly or pussy willow

Sphagnum moss

Mexican beach pebbles

•Choose a container and fill it part way with potting soil. Make sure you use a special soil mix for orchids, which includes bark chips for faster drainage. Regular soil will retain too much water and drown the roots.

•Place your plant or plants in the pot and fill it with more soil mix.

•Add a few branches of curly willow or pussy willow for contrasting texture.

•Cover the soil with sphagnum moss, which dresses up the dirt while maintaining moisture balance. Place a few Mexican beach pebbles on top as the finishing touch.

Fresh Avocado Facial Mask

Avocado is rich in natural oils and antioxidants, perfect for a mask to leave your skin silky smooth and your face feeling ready to smile.

1 avocado, peeled and pitted

Water

•Mash the avocado with a fork or puree it in the blender, adding water as needed to form a smooth paste.

•While in a hot bath, apply the mask all over your face. Leave on for 15–20 minutes.

•Gently wash the mask away with a cloth and refresh with a splash of cool water.

Herbal Eye Refresher

As a model I used this technique often—and guess what? I still do! This simple herbal treatment helps to reduce eye puffiness and is beautifully soothing after a long day's work.

2 chamomile tea bags

Warm water

•Steep the tea bags in warm water for about one minute to activate the herbs.

•Dip the tea bags into a glass of ice water and lay them on your closed eyes for 10–15 minutes.

•Relax (while drinking the chamomile tea, if you like).

vase variations

Decorative items such as vases might seem frivolous in the bathroom, but these are just the sort of accents that can warm up the space. Instead of using glass, try using an outdoor bucket, watering can, or copper kettle. If you don't have fresh flowers this week, cut some outdoor greens or, for a change, use the bucket to display your extra hand towels.

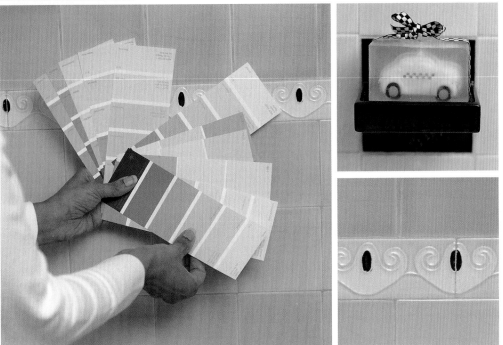

Spotlighting Beautiful Tile

Sometimes a room has a feature that's already so beautiful, making a style statement all its own, that you don't want to get in the way—just to help it along by adding finishing touches and making the space practical. That's how I felt about this tile bathroom in yellow, green, and black. I didn't want to detract from its original vintage charm, so I decided to keep my styling supplies in line with the tile's prominent colors, in order to draw attention to their beauty. I sought colors similar to my vintage tile, and I found it in these towels, rug, and a few other styling supplies.

Styling Tips

1 **Stylish Storage:** If you're lacking storage in your bathroom, choose a small cabinet to house your miscellaneous items. You'll also gain some additional space to style!

2 **Tidy Towels:** An easy way to spruce up your bathroom in minutes is to fold your towels into a tidy, colorful stack. Even if you don't have much space, you can arrange them in a way that minimizes clutter and maximizes impact. Lay the towel flat lengthwise and fold in both sides so that no rough edges are showing. Then fold top side down and bottom end up. Do the same with your washcloths.

Part III:
Creating Everyday Outdoor Style

7
Introduce Yourself: Styling Outdoor Entrances

8
Fresh Air: Styling Your Outdoor Rooms

9
Into the Elements: Styling the Garden

Chapter

Introduce Yourself: Styling Outdoor Entrances

7

come on in...

Saying Hello with Style

I knew a lot about Marilyn before I ever met her. My friend Sally and I pass her house every day during our morning walks. I love to see how the exterior of each home represents the unique personality of its inhabitants. Sally and I share a passion for real estate, and we exchange lively ideas about the neighborhood's scenes on our morning sojourn.

Every time we walked by Marilyn's house I would stop and admire the garden through the gate. I was fascinated by the constant changes that took place: an added architectural element, a stone rabbit, hanging baskets, a birdbath. The front yard and entrance areas of her home exuded a sense of magic and fantasy.

I especially loved Marilyn's front-gate arbor and front porch, with their parade of seasonal decorations. The person who lived here clearly cared deeply about her life, the people in it, and the statement she shared with the world.

Although I admired several seasons of creativity in Marilyn's garden, I had never actually seen Marilyn. I really wanted to meet this mystery figure. Then one day as Sally and I walked by, a woman and two young children emerged from the house and crossed the front yard.

I paused in my tracks. "Look, Sally, she has little ones."

I peeked in through the wrought-iron gate and waved at Marilyn and the children running across the lawn. (I found out later they were her granddaughters.) Marilyn waved back, and our friendship began.

What parts of your house are seen by the most people? Your entryways. From a simple door off a hall in an apartment complex to a full front yard with a porch or verandah, your entrance forms the first impression—the one that lasts.

My desire to meet Marilyn was sparked by the vignettes she created around the front of her house—a very important and yet often overlooked area. A few simple styling touches in entrance spaces can turn a nondescript house into a home with a smiling face.

I consider entrances a public relations tool. You might not think PR is important to you, but think again. If you take the trouble to return phone calls promptly, dress appropriately for an event, or send out holiday greetings, you're practicing public relations, which establishes continuity in relationships.

Why is personal PR important? Because it's a direct reflection of you and who you are! Many of us have worked hard to understand ourselves, and we care about expressing our identity accurately to the world. And so it is with the entrance to your home. You want it to make a welcoming statement that reflects the style of the people who live inside.

Of course there's no need to stick to the front door when you're styling entrances. Backdoors and guest-house doors, driveways and garages can all benefit from extra attention. Every entry can extend a welcome, and everyday styling makes this hello easy.

seasonal greetings:
fresh looks for any doorway

A doorway is a transition between dimensions. Closed, an external door is a barrier against the outside world; open, it invites the outside in. Styled with harmony in mind, the doorway can unite these two spaces by expressing the energy of both. All you have to do is let the season be your guide.

Spring, summer, winter, and fall are all great excuses to add personality to your doorway, and each season provides its own palette of colors, textures, and natural materials with which to work. Here, I used style scenarios based on the four seasons all around the house and arranged the front entry, a side or back door, a patio entry off the bedroom, and the entrance to a guest cottage.

Spring

Fresh Frame of Mind

Spring is the season of renewal, and even in California I can't wait to get outside to greet the return of warm breezes and longer days. Celebrate the spirit of sunshine and growth by styling your entries with a playful eye.

This moss square frame display was inspired by the joy of being a child in the spring—running outside after a long winter, gathering treasures as the natural world comes to life. A wonderfully whimsical way to mark the season.

Style-to: Moss Square Frame

Styling supplies:

Frame

Floral foam bricks

Hot glue gun

Sphagnum moss

Artificial butterflies, bugs, flowers,
    buttons, bows, whatever you like

Straight pins with colorful heads, or wire

One safety pin

Ribbon to hang (of a color similar to
    the items you're using)

• If you want more depth to your
frame, build it up by adding floral foam.
Trim the foam brick to the desired finished height of the frame. Starting at
the center of the brick, cut down at a
45-degree angle to shape the profile
of the foam and repeat on other side.
Next, miter the corners of the foam
bricks so that they meet evenly at each
corner. Glue the bricks to the frame
using hot glue.

• Spread glue over the top of the frame
or the added foam and place pieces
of the sphagnum moss to cover.

• Starting in one corner, attach your
items through the moss to the floral
foam with straight pins or wire (pins
with colorful heads work particularly
well as centers for the flowers). When
one corner is done, proceed to the op-
posite corner for balance, then start
filling in. It looks best if you don't fill
the entire frame.

• Tie the ribbon in a loop and secure it
to the back of the frame with a safety
pin. Add another piece of ribbon
around the middle bottom area of the
frame for visual balance. Hang.

a breath of spring

**When the traditional round wreath of winter comes down, why not change
shape along with the season? A square frame offers a geometrical change
of pace. This one is currently adding life to the glass-paned front door of
a guest cottage, but it would be equally charming on any door. Apartment
and condominium dwellers can use a moss square frame, wreath, or other
door hanging to quickly personalize the front entry, which can make a big
difference in an impersonal shared space. Keeping the statement seasonal
especially helps to liven up an indoor hallway.**

**For a touch of nostalgic charm, fill your frame with items that remind
you of your childhood, or include elements your own children have brought
you.**

Styling supplies:

Twig wreath or wire wreath frame

Wire

Two forsythia branches (real or artificial)

Wire clippers

• Lay the wreath frame on the table and place one forsythia branch on top at a time, wiring it to the wreath to hold. Note that real forsythia branches are usually quite pliable if they have just been cut, but if allowed to dry out they can become brittle and harder to work with.

• Continue laying branches in a circle around the wreath, fastening each with wire, until you feel it's full enough. The key here is simplicity!

TIP: Wreath frames are available at most craft stores and some garden and even fabric stores.

changeable pillows and wreath

Give your bench a new identity each season simply by changing the pillows and the wreath that hangs on the wall behind. Keep yours in touch with the times by picking two to three new colors each season to guide your choice of pillows and wall hanging. You might create a wall-mounted bouquet of dried flowers and reeds for fall, toss a warm throw on the bench in the winter, and search the house for pillows in pale pastels at the first sign of spring.

Summer

Bright Welcome Bench

A bench outside the door is both a friendly welcome to visitors and a great opportunity for styling. Whether it's a place for guests to wait or a respite on your postal carrier's route, an entrance bench is old-fashioned hospitality. The one on the front porch of my last home saw a lot of traffic from my Federal Express delivery woman—a well-earned moment of rest in her fast-paced day.

When summertime comes, I like to take my entryway color palette from the profusion of plants all around. *Bright* is the usual result, and it seems just the right welcome for this sun-drenched time of year. Red, yellow, and turquoise form the color scheme for this cheery seating spot, which sits on a bedroom patio that doubles as a back entry to the house. Whether luring you out of bed and into the morning sun or greeting backyard occupants, the pillows add summer exuberance to the simple wooden bench, and the wreath is the crowning touch.

Harvest Cart

Autumn is blessed by a harvest bounty of natural styling gifts. Every year I take the kids out to Lombardi Ranch, where there's a pumpkin patch complete with a scarecrow alley populated by bird-frightening figures designed by children from nearby schools. I usually load up the truck with a haul of pumpkins, gourds, and Indian corn; the prices are so good, I can get three times as much as I would if I bought the same thing in town—and there's lots of styling to do!

As the days turn crisp, I like to dress up my front door with a garden cart heaped with pumpkins, gourds, and corn to celebrate the harvest.

Fall

Styling Tips

1 **Surprise Flowers:** I love to mingle flowers with other types of plant material for contrast and softness. Here, I added sunflowers to my harvest cart. Not only do the colors harmonize perfectly, but the flowers will continue to look lovely as they dry.

2 **Hidden Height:** An inexpensive filler such as straw or hay enables you to give the illusion of abundance without having to buy out the farmers' market. If you don't have straw or hay on hand, fill the cart with anything handy—plastic pots turned upside down, milk crates, anything that weather won't damage but will fill the bottom and form a base for your display.

3 **A Touch of Green:** Variegated ivy is one of my favorite styling supplies. With green leaves shaped like stars tipped with white trim, ivy adds texture, trails with natural grace, and turns hard lines, like the edges of this cart, into soft falls of foliage.

4 **Indoor-Outdoor Table:** To extend your theme of harvest bounty from outside into the house, look for other items from the yard that mix well with your autumnal color palette—branches, wheat, grasses, and leaves in oranges, yellows, greens, burgundies, and browns—and put them on an indoor entry table, flanked by a few gourds. This pulls your entryway color palette right through the front door.

Style-to: Easy Globe Topiary

Topiary, or the art of clipping trees or shrubs into fanciful shapes, dates back to the hanging gardens of Babylon. From basic contours you conquered in geometry class to animals or even people, these plant sculptures can take whatever shapes the trimmer's imagination and skills might produce. Topiaries were also very popular in English gardens in formal shapes such as globes or pyramids.

To make a good topiary out of a tree, shrub, or hedge, the plant should be full enough to prune. Juniperus chinensis, an evergreen with upright pyramidal form and tightly needled branches, is perfect to cut into topiary because of its dense foliage.

Styling supplies:

Evergreen tree
Paper, pencil, and masking tape
Measuring tape
Pruning shears

• Start by sketching the shape of your tree on a piece of paper.

• Next, draw three circles stacked vertically within the outline of the tree, leaving a bit of space in between.

• Using the diagram as your guide, measure from the top of the shrub or tree to the bottom of the greenery and then divide the distance into three even sections. Mark the bottom of each section with a piece of masking tape.

• Working from the top down, start clearing the area at each tape mark by gently pruning the greenery. Your goal is to leave two to eight inches of bare tree trunk in between each globe.

• Once you have divided the sections clearly, start to shape each globe, leaving the bottom one a bit larger and getting smaller as you go up.

• Keep your topiaries trimmed up to maintain their shape. Don't worry if you overtrim; they grow back!

Festive Front Entry

Winter is a time for holiday celebrations and getting the home ready to receive family and friends. Although wreaths, lights, ribbons, and bows are often used to cheer up the dark time of year, few people think to style with live plants during the dead of winter—but why not? Your beds may be frozen, but potted conifers bring greenery and living energy directly to your entryway, and they last the entire season. By the time the plants outgrow their pots, the ground will be thawed and you can plant them in the yard for years of future pleasure.

Styling Tips

1 **Topiary Trio:** "Grouping" is the style principle that makes these three pots of junipers and cypress on each side of the front door so interesting. The symmetrical layout and carefully trimmed topiary lend formality, while the variety of color, shape, texture, and height creates contrast to catch the eye. I've used *Juniperus chinensis,* an evergreen that's great for topiary; *Cypressus arizonica,* with a symmetrical pyramidal form of blue-gray foliage on compact branches; and New Blue Tamarix Juniper, or *Juniperus sabina,* which has blue foliage and provides a nice complement to the other two conifers.

2 **Berry Wreath Trim:** In addition to decorating the door, you can also lay a wreath around the base of one of the conifer pots to add color to the foreground of your entryway tableau. Simply lay strands of berries around the base of the pot and work them into a wreath shape, then wire the branches together to hold them in place. The red berry accents unite the entry space and create a warm winter welcome.

This past year I switched to artificial berries for holiday displays because I was nervous about my baby putting poisonous berries in her mouth. Nobody could tell the difference and I gained peace of mind.

3 **Visual Variety:** Just as you may use a variety of spices to make your holiday baking special, spice up your entryway by mixing and matching pots in different colors, materials, and sizes. Experiment until the results are exciting but harmonious.

4 **Read the Label:** A plant tag is full of pertinent information, from the species' idiosyncrasies to a recipe for proper care. When choosing plants at the nursery, take a minute to read the tags and target varieties that will work in your environment. Slip tags into your Style File for easy reference.

before

*M*any people have some sort of entry area without obvious potential—a slab of concrete driveway, a nondescript patio, the garage entrance that serves as your daily welcome home while the front door goes virtually unused. The good news is that you can style these entrances too—even if you've got car clutter or a poorly designed space to deal with—and doing so provides a great example of the transformative power of looking at space with the eyes of an everyday stylist. In fact, one good Sunday foray turned my own piece of concrete jungle into a favorite part of the house.

concrete jungle:
creating great driveway entrances

I love going to Pasadena's Rose Bowl Swap Meet, held the second Sunday of every month, and lucky for me it's only ten minutes away. On this fine day I arrived home with no more than I could carry.

"You did well," Bobby said with a grin when I walked in the door. By that he meant I didn't buy much.

"I did great!" I dashed upstairs to see if my purchases would work in the bathroom.

"By the way," I shouted down the stairs, "someone will be dropping off a few more things." I imagined his smile fading as I styled the space around my new mirror.

A few hours later, we were playing with Hailey by the front window when a small truck pulled up. I passed Bobby the baby and headed for the door.

"Come on out and meet Paul Moyer," I told him. "He's from Kansas so he may know some of your family."

As Bobby followed me out the front door, he could see that the small truck was pulling a 14-foot trailer filled to the brim with old salvage goods—rusting farm equipment, weathered fence gates, buckets, bins, ladders, and tools. He gasped for air.

"Paul runs a salvage company and trucks this stuff all the way from Kansas to the Rose Bowl every month—can you believe it? This is straight from your hometown."

Bobby looked sick.

I patted his cheek. "Don't worry, this isn't all mine."

A faint smile broke through—until Paul started unloading my treasures. Three rusty old rakes and two rusty old chairs. I held up the next item.

"Very special," I said.

Bobby stared blankly, so I found a more appreciative audience.

"See Hailey? A cob rake—specially designed for cornfields."

She cooed with excitement.

"But we don't grow corn," Bobby muttered.

You'd think after eleven years of marriage he'd be used to it, but he still doesn't know whether to laugh or cry. I encouraged him to reminisce about Kansas with our new friend, then started to carry my haul to the backyard.

While all this was going on, the realtor selling my neighbor's house walked over to introduce himself.

"I noticed you were dumping some things and I wondered if you could ask your guy to take one table the Salvation Army forgot."

"I'm not dumping," I said, "I just bought this stuff. What table?"

Now I had two men looking at me in horror, but without another word the realtor led me to my neighbor's front porch and a green vintage metal table that I knew would be perfect in front of my backyard garage studio.

"I'll take it," I said. "Could you help me bring it over?"

The next thing poor Bobby saw was the realtor and me passing by with what to his eyes was just one more piece of clutter for our new house, a lovely 1927 Spanish bungalow with next to no storage space. But I knew that as I styled, what looked like clutter would become a unique entryway that would make even Bobby smile.

Driveway Studio Entrance

When I converted my garage into a home studio, the grand entrance to my new creative space was a hot slab of driveway. My first thought was to tear up the concrete and plant a garden, but my contractor told me that since it was a low spot, water might seep in and under the garage; a traditional garden was out. With a few ideas in my head I went to the Rose Bowl that day determined to see the full possibilities of my driveway entrance unfurl.

Enter my flea market finds: First I took the pieces of picket fence I'd bought from Paul, altered them a bit, and sectioned off the space, adding potted pink hydrangeas for a punch of color. Inside the fence, I put the table I got from the neighbors, arranged the rakes and ladder behind it, added the two old metal chairs, and *voilà*—instant grand entrance!

I collect precious memories like that crazy afternoon with Bobby, Paul, and the realtor along with my outdoor styling treasures. Now when my friends come over and ask me about the rakes poised in front of the stucco wall next to my studio (a nice clean white backdrop), or the green table where we sip lemonade, I have a hilarious story to tell. I still laugh out loud every time I think of those guys' faces.

Everyday Styling Basic: Personal, Not Perfect

Style is exciting. Style tells stories. Style has personality. But it need not be perfect. When something is too flawless—for instance, an immaculately trimmed garden or an absolutely symmetrical living room devoid of personal possessions—it can lose the very appeal you're trying to achieve. Perfection can seem stiff, phony, inhuman. Think about an old man's face, wrinkled and weathered with the history, experience, and wealth of his life—this is a face with character, one that's fascinating to behold.

Similarly, the style of your space should reflect the rich details of your passions and personality, not some ideal of perfection. It's often the mismatched item, the asymmetrical grouping, or surprise element that brings style to life. Think personal, not perfect, and watch real beauty emerge.

great garage entries

Do you park your car in the garage and enter the house directly from there with no warmer welcome than a few trashcans and a cobwebby lawnmower in the way? Even if your entryway is hidden from outside eyes, if you walk through it, spruce it up with personal touches that will light up your arrival even after the longest day.

Every year after Christmas, my mother-in-law, Cally, takes the wreath from over her fireplace and hangs it on the inside garage wall, where it dries and gives her a great welcome home every day. Any number of small touches can help beat the garage entry blues—an antique ladder hung on the wall and strung with dried flowers, a piece of standing picket fence to camouflage the recycling bins, a door painted a pretty color, a favorite picture from inside the house, or the kids' artwork to create a colorful mural.

Style-to: Picket Fence Perimeter

When styling a garage entry, driveway, or patio, defining the perimeter is the first and most important step. The picket fence trick I used might work for you, too.

Styling supplies:

New or old picket fence

3 wood 1 x 4s the length of every section of fence you have

2 10–12-inch-long 1 x 4s for each section

Drill

Screws and screwdriver

Paint

• Measure the entrance space you want to enclose.

• Find or purchase the lengths of fencing you need. (These generally come precut, so be prepared to be flexible and know your possible parameters.)

• Purchase the 1 x 4s you'll need to build the stands for the fence. (You can have the lumber yard cut the wood to size.)

• Using a drill and long screws, create the three sides of your stand (the fence will be the fourth side) with one long 1 x 4 and the two shorter pieces.

• Screw the other two long pieces to the three-sided box as slats to form the bottom.

• Attach the open end of the stand to the uprights of your fence to form the fourth side, with the slats on the bottom.

• Repeat steps 4 to 6 for every piece of fence.

• Paint the fence and stand the same color to unify the look.

• Place the fence pieces to section off the space, and, finally, add potted plants to the boxes you've built that complement your color scheme.

Note: If you don't have fencing, you can use a line of pots and plant material in different heights to define a perimeter. In addition to creating a boundary, your "living fence" adds greenery and color to the space.

Mint Syrup Lemonade

By adding two vintage chairs to the table I inherited from the neighbors, I gained a sweet little entryway seating area where I can come outside and catch some rays or sip lemonade with a friend. This recipe brings to mind an endless Southern summer afternoon, although I drink it all year round.

Syrup:

1 cup water

8 tablespoons sugar

6 sprigs fresh mint, plus additional leaves for garnish (optional)

Peel of 2 lemons

1 cinnamon stick, 3 inches long

• In a small saucepan, stir together the water, sugar, mint, lemon peel, and cinnamon stick. Bring to a simmer over medium heat and cook, stirring occasionally, 10 minutes. Pour the syrup through a strainer into a small bowl. Let cool about 10 minutes.

Lemonade:

5 lemons

1 quart water

• Squeeze the juice of the lemons into a pitcher and add water. Then add enough syrup to sweeten. Taste as you stir. Serve over ice.

vintage tools

Vintage tools have so much character, recalling times past when work was an art form and everything was done by hand. They make great styling items, hung on a wall or displayed in unexpected places like pieces of art.

colorized hydrangeas

You can change the color of some hydrangeas like magic just by adjusting the pH of your soil. Hortensia hydrangea *(Hydrangea macrophylla)* will turn blue if the soil is on the acid side. To achieve the necessary pH level, between 4.5 and 5.5, prepare the soil when planting with two pounds of sulfur and peat moss, then fertilize yearly with an acid fertilizer, according to directions. To turn flowers pink to light red, the soil should be neutral to slightly alkaline—pH 6.5 to 7.5. Scatter ground limestone around the plant if the color isn't pink enough, but take it easy: if pH levels rise above 7.5, you'll get faded leaves and poor growth.

Fresh Air: Styling Your Outdoor Rooms

8

up on the roof...

Elevated Outdoor Living

Every chance they get during the summer months, an otherwise moderately sane New York City family I know schlepps food, plates, silverware, buckets of ice, and sodas up a spindly ladder and through a narrow hatch onto the roof of their brownstone to cook dinner on a tiny old gas-fired grill—ignoring the comfortable, spacious, well-equipped apartment below. Mysteriously, those of their friends who have witnessed this odd behavior clamor to be invited along, often calling them on some flimsy pretext and then asking (by the way), "When is the next rooftop barbecue?"

But, I'll confess, as I write this, I am not sitting at my comfortable, spacious, well-equipped desk but outside on my patio (thank heavens for a laptop), where I'm at the mercy of bugs, breezes, and incontinent or insouciant birds. Who am I to talk about sanity?

When I was finally dragged up onto Peter and Rita's roof—and once I got over the initial awe of seeing Manhattan spread out below me—I marveled at what my friends had done to break up a space no bigger than a small California patio. The walls were covered with vines that suggested a country garden. A European café table, complete with umbrella, sat in one corner, perfect for cocktails or dinner for four or five. On the adjacent roof, a neighbor's large glass table was available for bigger affairs. The elevator housing became a sylvan nook with a log bench nestled among the vines, and on the other side of the elevator were a grill and prep table in their own little enclosure. A few feet of empty space led to the rail along the front of the building, giving the kids a place to play and drawing the eye out and up to the dramatic view. I could easily see why Peter and Rita left their well-appointed apartment on soft summer nights. They'd created an entire home up on the roof with rooms for many activities, with Manhattan at their feet and the stars and sky above.

Outdoor living is in our blood, our bones, and our genes. I'll bet the very first cavewoman couldn't wait each morning to crawl out of her smoky cave and into the open air, saber-toothed tigers notwithstanding. And once she got there, she probably rearranged the rocks.

But the outdoors is a big place and can be overwhelming. I often hear from homeowners who look out their windows and feel as if their controllable world ends at the patio perimeter. After that, it's just one big jungle out there, an undifferentiated mass of greenery, grass, and dirt.

features to make the most of your outdoor space.

For instance, if you style your outdoor entertaining area—perhaps the patio, deck, or porch—with the dining room and kitchen in mind, you'll end up with lovely tables and a functional cooking area. Once you start to view children's play areas as mirror images of the indoor family room or playroom, you'll resist the temptation to let chaos rule just because you're outside. And where's your outdoor living room? Set up some seating areas separate from the dining space for intimate chats and reading. To break the psychological boundaries of the walls of the house, bring indoor elements such as drapes, pillows, mirrors, or candelabra out to the patio or yard—perhaps even a rug to soften the concrete floor or add a patch of color to the lawn. Soon, you'll find you're just as comfortable outside as inside on any nice day, doubling the value of your real estate and enhancing the pleasure of the great outdoors.

Treat your outdoor rooms as

This endless expanse doesn't mesh with our natural instinct to create personal space, and for many people, it's a daunting prospect to take it on.

My show, *Surprise Gardener*, is about transforming a yard in a single day within a reasonable budget, tackling *one space at a time*—and this is the magic trick. We simply look around, assess what we have to work with, and delineate a number of different areas that will be useful and beautiful for the way the owners live. There may be a foreground— a patio set up for effortless entertaining. A middle area, perhaps a swing set on the grassy lawn or a sandbox for kids. To the side, a seating area under a shady tree. The principle behind this divide-and-conquer approach to fresh-air living is an everyday styling concept I call "outdoor rooms."

The Outdoor Room Attitude

Breaking down your outdoor spaces into "rooms" lets you style each one according to its individual purpose and identity. The best way to do this is to think of literal rooms in the house and translate their essential

The Indoor-Outdoor Continuum

Indoor items such as furniture, rugs, curtains, cushions, and pillows can add comfort and style to your outdoor rooms. However, many indoor furnishings aren't made to take a beating from sun, wind, rain, and dirt even during the temperate season. While most outdoor furniture and pillows are made from materials that can withstand the weather, delicate items brought out to jazz up an outdoor room are best brought back inside by the evening's end.

From the thousands of homeowners I've talked to over the years, the most common items on people's wish lists are outdoor entertaining areas to accommodate gatherings with friends and family, play spaces for kids that look as attractive to adults as they do to their young users, and tranquil spots for relaxing or reading. Start with these three concepts for styling a yard and see how you gain a tremendous sense of spaciousness. Your home is no longer limited by the walls, but stretches out across the yard toward the horizon and the sky above.

an integral part of your home.

al fresco fun:
styling outdoor entertaining areas

Outdoor entertaining has a special magic all its own. Whether laid back or elegant, outside celebrations add the beauty of nature, the spontaneity of open space, the invigorating effect of fresh air to the party. Decks, patios, and porches make great settings for outdoor events, but you might prefer a banquet table in the middle of the lawn or a party table in the corner of your garden for more festive times. Whatever space you choose, once you style your outdoor entertaining room, planning a party or a family picnic or just slipping outside to enjoy a solo sandwich al fresco is a breeze.

As always, keep function in mind as you decide on the form of your outdoor entertaining rooms. Consider the different requirements of a party, a small family meal, or sitting with a friend over morning coffee. Think about softening hard lines and bringing the indoors out to make things feel warm and personable. Also keep in mind that you want to clearly identify your outdoor rooms by making a statement with each that separates one area from another.

If you think of your outdoor entertaining area as a place for people to interact with nature and each other, the styling process is as natural as the blossoming of spring.

Poolside Patio

When we bought this house I knew this pool area would be a great spot for outdoor entertaining with just a few styling touches.

I started by enclosing the arbor with drapes to create an elegant living and dining room right at the water's edge. Then, focusing on the fuchsia of the bougainvillea, I pulled the color through the area with potted plants, cut flowers, and a few accent pillows. The color cue for the curtains is found in the trim on the table.

open-air privacy

Adding drapes to a plant-covered arbor is a great way to create a very private outdoor room with sweeping soft lines you may not have seen in your yard before. It's up to you whether you open the curtains to take in the view or keep them closed for an intimate dinner à deux.

Style-to: Draped Arbor

Styling supplies:

Curtains

Curtain rods and hardware

Pencil

Drill

Screwdriver

• Space out your curtain rod brackets along the top of the arbor opening and mark the drill holes with a pencil.

• Drill as marked and screw the brackets into the wood.

• Mount the rod, evenly placing the curtain rings between the brackets.

• Hang the drapes.

You can also hang the drape directly on the rod, but I like the easy sliding action of the rings. Rings with clips, such as these, make it easy to take the drapes down to store in the winter months.

Note: If you're shopping for new curtains and rods to fit your arbor, measure the distances you need to cover before you go and note them in your Portable Style File.

Styling Tips

1 **Vines—Nature's Drapes:** Vines add a fascinating vertical dimension to the garden, and it's easy to get yours started twining toward the sky.

There are four principal types of vines, defined by how they attach. Vines with disc-shaped suckers, such as *Ficus repens pumila*, will scale the wall of your house for a European villa effect. Climbing rose, or *Mandevilla*, have no inherent fastener and need to be attached to walls or trellises. Then there are twining vines, such as star jasmine, that wrap themselves around objects. Tendril vines, such as morning glory, have offshoots that will willingly grab onto anything and work well on chain link fences. Wisteria, bougainvillea, or grapes are good bets to drape your arbor or pergola walls.

2 **Bottle Collection Centerpiece:** For a centerpiece with the free spirit of the outdoors, collect old or new bottles in different

sizes, shapes, and colors. Group them together and fill each one with a different flower or sprig of greenery from the garden.

3 **Patio Table Dressing:** To style a stunning patio table, choose a color palette from those in your tile, table, or surrounding plant

material. I picked up the beige, turquoise and mustard from my table, and the fuschia from the bougainvillea. Tie the look together

with place mats and napkins, glassware, dishes, pillows, and additional plants in the same set of hues.

Birthday Lawn Party

In my visits to America's backyards I've noticed a common problem: plenty of lawn, but often no patio. Even if you have a patio or deck, the festivities of some big events—a daughter's wedding, child's birthday, or parents' fiftieth anniversary—won't fit. How can you set up the plain old yard so that it has a special sense of place? The answer is to style an outdoor room right in the middle of the lawn!

Here, I created a festive party spot for my daughter's birthday in my friends' front yard. I put up an entryway to add height and define the perimeter, backed by a table full of goodies to entice the guests to enter. For a larger affair you could add more tables and archways, creating a magical village that transports your lawn to a different world.

Blue, lime, and purple make up my party color palette. You might try white for a wedding shower, pink or blue or yellow for a baby shower, or black and orange for a Halloween party.

Styling Tip

1 **Party Color Palette:** Color can set the tone of the party—and for this one I took my inspiration from a purple stroller. (I love purple, and, okay, I admit it, I had a three-toned purple bedroom growing up.) When I spotted a package of lime, blue, and purple bows, they looked so good together that I used the trio of colors as the basis for all my styling supplies—wrapping, netting, and flowers. Filling the stroller with wrapped presents turns it into a birthday sleigh.

A specific color scheme is a great help when searching for styling supplies. Refer to your Style File for fresh combinations and finish off the look with an extra accent color here and there. I happened to have some leftover orange tissue, and I liked the brightness it brought to the table, peeking out from goody bags. Don't forget the cut flowers!

Style-to: Stay-Put Fabric Tablecloth

Here are two tricks for outdoor table-cloths: Don't limit yourself to paper or plastic just because you're outside. And once you've picked your cloth, make sure it stays in place even in a passing breeze. In this case, I had a common party problem: The table was bigger than most tablecloths. No worries—you can make your own tablecloth from a fabric that matches your theme and affix it directly to the table with this simple style-to.

Styling supplies:

Cotton fabric base in your color
     palette, at least twice the length
     of your table plus four times the
     height from tabletop to the ground
A second piece of draping fabric
     (rayon, poly chiffon) in a
     contrasting color
Rolled tape (optional)
Pins

• Lay the base fabric out on the table and iron it smooth. (It's fun to iron outdoors, and sparks great conversation with people who pass by! Just plug your iron into an outdoor extension cord.)

• Place the fabric over the table and measure so that it hits the ground on both ends, then cut it at that point, setting the second piece aside.

• Tape the first piece in place so that it covers the legs of the table in the front and drapes down to the ground on both ends.

• Lay the second piece partly over the first one, to cover the back legs of the table, hanging evenly to the ground on both ends. If you like, you can use double-face or rolled tape to secure this to the first piece.

• Finish by draping your contrasting fabric in front and pinning it at both ends of the table, letting the ends fall down to the ground.

Style-to: Bamboo Archway

Styling supplies:

Duct tape

4 tent stakes

4 bamboo poles of equal length, about
   8–10 feet tall

String

Screwdriver

Step stool

Nylon netting in one base color, about
   24 feet long (I used peacock)

2 pieces of nylon tulle (finer netting),
   one in the same base color and the
   other in a complementary color,
   each about 24 feet long (I used
   peacock and periwinkle)

• Securely tape the tent stakes to the
bottom of the poles to act as anchors,
leaving 3–4 inches of stake free at the
bottom to go into the ground.

• Stick the poles into the ground, cross-
ing them about a foot from the top,
then tie them together securely with
string where they cross. If necessary,
use a screwdriver to make holes in the
dirt before driving in the poles.

• Drape the nylon netting through the
two V's you created with the poles to
create an arch, allowing the top to
hang down a little and the sides to fall
evenly to the ground.

• Repeat this procedure with each of
the two pieces of nylon tulle.

• For extra style, tie a bow on top of
each side using a piece of nylon tulle.

• Adjust the netting and tulle so that it
covers the poles and drapes nicely to
the bottom.

Note: If it's a bit windy, use string to
stake the structure as you would a tent.

Styling Tips

1 **Dramatic Draping:** I am a devotee of draping material to add dimension and élan to formerly flat surfaces. If you keep fabric

on hand you can pull out a similar or contrasting color to drape any table in loads of additional style.

2 **Plastics Made Perfect:** Simplify serving and continue the color scheme by wrapping each set of plastic ware in a paper

napkin and tying it up with a ribbon, both selected from your color palette.

3 **Simplified Stylish Gift Wrap:** Wrapping a number of gifts at once can test your creative limits, but here's a tip to simplify

the process and make your gift table look great: Buy just a couple of solid wraps and gift bags in colors from your theme, an

assortment of ribbons in different textures, widths, and complementary colors, and a package of assorted tissue paper. Stick to

your selected solids for the main wrapping, creating a nice continuity of design, then mix and match ribbons and tissue paper accents

for interest.

4 **Sweet-Looking Treats:** Food is a fantastic styling prop, and sweets in a broad spectrum of colors can serve as edible accents

for your party table. Select an assortment of shapes, sizes, and colors from your palette and arrange them in a variety of dishes.

Grouping by type tends to heighten the effect, as with these green, red, and blue swizzle twists in separate turquoise cups.

*D*o you remember as a child coming across some enchanted outdoor space that seemed to be a world of its own? A cluster of trees with a hidden clearing within, a bend in the stream harboring a sheltered pool that became a playground for your dolls-turned-mermaids, an unexpected cave? Whether in the woods, on the beach, or in someone's backyard, what those spaces shared was a sense of intimacy, a place that you could make your own—and then use to make your own magic.

child's play:
styling outdoor playrooms

Kids need a place where their imaginations can run free and where they can play without worry about breaking anything. I've found that it doesn't take much to make kids happy (though mine aren't teenagers yet). Just creating a small fort, a pretty sandbox, a special spot all their own can make a big difference to little ones. If you have kids or pint-size visitors, an outdoor playroom is a must—and everyday styling can keep it fun.

Children get bored at least as easily as adults, and their spaces need energy, rejuvenation, and change just like the grown-up parts of the house and yard. Adding and changing that little something here and there in the play area helps teach kids that they can keep creating and bettering their environment.

Get out there with your kids and have a ball styling spaces to play in. You may find that if you provide supplies, they'll supply the style. Try setting up a small table and giving the children a fun mix of miscellaneous dishes and linens so that they can create their own setting and call you out for tea. Invite them to pick some flowers or greenery. You're sure to get a kick out of the results—and they'll love to see your smile.

Swingin' Swing Set

Swings are just the thing for a child's outdoor play area, but they can take up a lot of space and look pretty drab to adults. Whether you have a full swing set or a rustic wood plank hung with rope from a tree, styling your swing with some flowers offers a nice surprise and a pleasing view from outside or inside the house.

Style-to: Camouflage Fort

Styling supplies:

2 bamboo or tent poles, 4–5 feet high, one 2 feet taller than the other

Tent stakes and orange cord

Camouflage fabric (4 yards of a 56–60 inch-wide roll)

Loose change or pebbles

• Take the taller pole and stake it into the ground as the front part of the fort. Find the center of one end of the fabric and place it over the pole, allowing for some excess to drop over the front of the pole.

• Wrap the fabric securely around the top of the pole with the orange cord (easy to see) and tie it off, leaving six feet of cord hanging down for staking.

• Repeat the same process for the back shorter pole to establish the ridge of the fort.

• For each side, grab the fabric about a foot off the ground and wrap it around a quarter or pebble, tying with cord to form a grommet. Leave the excess cord.

• Make a loop at the other end of the cord, slip it over a stake, pull the fabric taut, and push the stake into the ground. Repeat on all sides.

Styling Tips

1 **Style Supply Shopping:** For your safari fort, check out your nearest army surplus store for blankets, lanterns, canteens, and other cool, genuine-issue fort supplies that kids love.

2 **Love Bugs:** Both boys and girls love collecting bugs of all kinds, so stock your fort with a bug condo or two and some nets. This will keep the kids busy for hours of fun. Don't forget an evening firefly hunt!

Safari Camp

Kids love forts and I build one for Hutton any chance I get, inside and out, with pillows, sheets, towels, and some ingenious engineering. An inexpensive tent or an appropriately hung tarp is the foundation needed for your own backyard safari camp. The rest of the magic is in the styling supplies. Think camp stools and a table, a few pith helmets, a lantern, and butterfly nets.

This fort can have any theme you like—just use different types of fabric and styling supplies. For instance, move from safari to a mermaid's retreat with gauzy netting and a wading pool.

Today's Playhouse

A playhouse can take on many roles, from mission control for an elaborate adventure game to a place for club meetings to a mini-version of a grown-up house. My goal here was to bring the classic game of playing house to life, with a seating area, dishes, even a telephone that looked like the real thing. Restyle the playhouse as a space capsule, a log cabin, or a Parisian pied-à-terre as the kids get tired of the look or inspired by new ideas.

Styling Tips

1 **Junior Stylist:** Think of your playhouse as a place to let children create and style, teaching self-expression at an early age. Encourage the young residents to move the furniture around, hang curtains, stencil the floor, have a tea party, display collections, and put up their own works of art. When it's time for a big change, repaint and restyle. And no matter how enthusiastic you may become about the space, don't inadvertently stifle their creativity by overriding their styling decisions with yours.

A playhouse can instill creative habits, good organizational skills, and a flair for styling a happy home—or submarine, artist's studio, or whatever today's space may be.

2 **Pride of Ownership:** It's important for kids to have not only a special space, but sovereignty over what goes on there. Imagine if someone controlled how you handled all your possessions—it would drive you batty! Children will surprise you with the level of responsibility they can reach when you loosen up the reins. Styling is a great place to start.

Begin by teaching young children the value of work and the independence it brings. Start them earning and saving money from household or garden chores worth a few dollars—and then let the fun begin! It's off to garage sales to gather a few dishes, toys, perhaps a little chair. Back home, kids will be eager to take treasures bought with their own money and start styling, imagining, creating their own little lives and dreaming ever bigger dreams.

light your child's creative spark

Children are incredibly creative. When we're young, we style with a free spirit because we have yet to be out in the world and see any of our ideas shot down. Unfortunately, the spark of imagination is fragile, and most people get quantifiably less creative as they grow up.

If you have children, encourage their creative spirit and their joy in life's great adventure. Many of our society's important figures remember someone along the way who understood their sensibility and valued their personal flair. Share your everyday styling attitude with your kids early on and all the way through their teens, and their creativity will flourish for life. How do I know? Because my own mother planted the seeds in me that blossomed into everyday styling, and not a day goes by without my thanks for this life-affirming gift.

before

sit back and relax: styling outside seating areas

There's something about sitting outside that's very different from kicking back on the living room couch. The sound of birdsong, the butterflies flitting by, the gentle touch of the breeze, the unexpected hummingbird hovering in the trees—the spontaneous beauty of this world can help you unwind and reset your mind. Outdoor seating areas offer a soul-pleasing mix of civilization and nature's serenity, a spot to stop doing and *be*. To read that romance novel you've been saving. Catch up with a friend who's dropped by. Entice the guests at your patio party to come out into the yard and whisper secrets or steal kisses. Or simply to sit very still and admire your beautiful garden that has burst into bloom. Style some delightful sitting rooms in your backyard, and watch how these way stations beckon to all who pass by.

Magic Lantern Alcove

An outdoor sitting room can be so much more than a chair. In this yard, I found a white wrought-iron loveseat just waiting for some additions to create an enchanting alcove: a chair, rug, pillows, colorful paper lanterns, and butterflies on stakes. The indoor elements contribute to the cozy effect, while the lanterns add a magical, Arabian Nights nuance.

Styling Tips

1 **The Power of Three:** Whether I'm hanging paper lanterns, planting, or arranging flowers or greens, I like to group in threes. Why? Because of the interplay this odd number offers—the loose asymmetry that frees the eye from formal bounds.

2 **Surprising Stripes:** Stripes are always cheerful and can pack extra punch in the garden, where they provide contrast with the less organized lines of nature. In this alcove I mixed stripes, seen in the lanterns and rug, with solid and floral print pillows in the same selection of colors for a cheerful scene against the background of green.

3 **Sociable Seating Arrangements:** Many outdoor seating areas seem designed for solo contemplation—a single bench can provide a tranquil spot for retreat. But what if you want a place for conversation? Simply add a chair and a few cushions, and suddenly the set-up is sociable.

efore

Baker's Rack Vertical Garden

A wall or fence makes a well-suited backdrop for a seating area, but many look plain or drab, especially if on a patio without surrounding plant material. In such a case I like to add nature to the equation to provide a focal point and bring the seating area to life, perhaps with some winding vines, a large potted plant or, in this case, a vertical garden.

If you're accustomed to seeing baker's racks stacked with loaves of bread, it may not have entered your head to make a potted-plant garden out of one instead. Load the tiers of an old baker's rack with a variety of plants in different pots and planters, and you've got a surprise garden that rises to new heights. Add a couple of chairs to draw the eye to the plant display, and a stretch of empty wall becomes an instant room.

Styling Tips

1 **Mixed Materials:** Add interest to your baker's rack garden by mixing glass containers with hardy terracotta and round with rectangular shapes, using the color palette of the flowering plant material to tie the look together. Lavenders and pinks set the tone for this marriage of different materials.

2 **Conversation Nook:** To create an outdoor conversation area, configure the chairs or sofas so that they face each other to ease interaction and define the space. Try this anywhere—a patio, front porch, balcony, or side yard—to keep the lines of communication open.

3 **Foot-Friendly Foundation:** The rug really makes this space an outdoor room by providing common ground and warming up the concrete. These rugs are inexpensive and washable, so why not bring indoor comfort out and underfoot?

Meditative Retreat

The serene simplicity of Zen philosophy inspired this single chair flanked by a graceful stalk display. This arrangement can add atmosphere to any outdoor space but is particularly well suited for smaller spots such as a condominium patio, balcony, or front porch. If you like, move the display indoors to place alongside a small tabletop water feature for a mini indoor garden.

Everyday styling is about expanding your life and making the most of your home. When you use styling techniques to create appealing, activity-based areas for outdoor living—whether in a backyard, atop a brownstone roof, or on an apartment balcony—you break beyond the walls of your house to tap into the outside world.

Style-to: Zen Stalks Display

Styling supplies:

Container

Floral foam

Knife

Natural or artificial green stalks (if you go natural it's nice to pick something that will dry gracefully so you don't have to water)

River rocks

Mood moss, sphagnum moss, or baby's tears

• Choose a container from those you have on hand, or get a new one to bring another look into your space.

• Cut a piece of floral foam to fill the inside of the container. It's fine if you need to cut additional pieces to fit; no one will see them.

• Place your stalks by pushing them into the foam. I'm using artificial ones because they look so real and last forever. Group the stalks in odd numbers (I chose a single grouping of three).

• Cover the foam with Mexican beach pebbles or small river rocks from the garden supply store (you can get them in gray or white). Add a little greenery here and there to soften the look of the base. Sphagnum or mood moss will last quite a while and doesn't require watering. For a special occasion or nice fresh touch, pick some fresh greenery from the garden to slip between the rocks. It will only last a few days, but just pull it out when it starts to look bedraggled.

Chapter

Into the Elements: Styling the Garden

9

natural balance...

Five Elements to Garden Harmony

I once met a wise old man. He was a garden designer but didn't call

himself that. He worked as a hands-on gardener, so you wouldn't know

he was "designing" unless you noticed how the gardens he tended were

transformed over time, gradually changing with the season, ever more

interesting with each day he spent working on the space. I sometimes

followed him around while he trimmed and pruned a neighbor's yard and

we'd chat about China (where he was from) and what he was doing

while he worked.

I complimented him on his gardens, on how they always had a

special serenity, clarity, and quiet natural beauty.

"Your gardens are so beautiful," I said. "What's your magic?"

He smiled. "It's not magic, it's traditional Chinese science. Look."

He pointed to a small rock garden. "Earth."

Then he cupped his hand to his ear and I heard it, too—a wind

chime in a fruit tree. "Wind."

He nodded toward a burbling fountain. "Water."

He raised his eyes to the torches strategically placed around the

grounds. "Fire."

Finally, he gestured to the green, growing plant life all around us. "Wood."

I looked again and suddenly realized that there really was science underlying his artistic creations—the natural elements of ancient cosmology—earth, wind, water, fire, and wood.

I felt as if blinders had suddenly been stripped from my eyes. The natural world *is* about balance, the interplay between elements. To someone raised in a time and place in which a yard was defined as dirt and grass, this was a revelation.

The garden is an active, vital place, where plants follow their individual cycles day after day through the year's seasons of growth, dormancy, and rebirth. But the most exciting gardens are more than greenery, they use all of nature's elements in a singular mix that inspires your sense

Nature is about balance, the

of style. The steps in this chapter will help you to identify these key elements and put them into play according to your personal vision. You will be turning your yard into a garden of delight, and revealing the green thumb you may never have known you had. Are you ready to get out into the elements and let your garden style emerge?

Tapping the Natural Source

You may have heard about feng shui, the ancient Chinese tradition of enhancing energy in the environment. Feng shui's principles are based on finding the right balance between the elements of nature, just as my gardener friend described, so that people can live in harmony with the land. The central concept is that nature is the essential source of energy, and we can enjoy better prosperity and health by maximizing its flow.

Well, what better place to tap this natural energy source than in

the garden? A thriving environment is your front line in achieving good feng shui, positive energy, or whatever you care to call it, in your home's domain.

A garden is a living thing. Always in action, it's filled with growing plants reaching up, out, and all around; rain falling gently down; wind riffling through on its way to distant destinations; light streaming earthward and bouncing back up to illuminate all it touches. All this energy is available to invigorate your home and enliven each outdoor moment.

Plants can seem a bit more complicated to style than other features of the garden, or, for that matter, interiors—who ever heard of a chair wilting, or an ottoman overgrowing a whole room? But this living quality is the very thing that rewards your efforts so richly. Those of you who already spend time tending to your plants and working in the garden

know what I'm talking about. There is an uplifting of the spirit that occurs when one is down in the dirt that cannot easily be explained. The wonder of seeing your bulbs come up in the spring or your tomatoes ripen on the vine is something that will bring even a high-powered executive to his knees—literally—just to experience the joy of it all.

Once you start giving your plants the love and attention they need to flourish, you'll find they return it with interest. I like to think of gardening as communication with the living world. It could be verbal (we've all heard of people who talk to their plants), but watering, feeding, deadheading, pruning, and adding garden elements that give your plants personality and show off their best attributes will get your message through as well. When you put time and heart into anything that matters, it expands, blossoms, and grows. And as plants grow, so do the people who tend them.

interplay between elements.

before

A garden that's nothing more than a grouping of plants seems dull because it lacks balance—add the soothing sound of trickling water, the warm glow of a well-placed lantern, a cheerful flag waving in the breeze, or a pathway tempting you forward, and you create life by generating an interplay of different elements. When I style the garden, I always try to complement the plants—wood—with the other elements of earth, wind, fire, and water. Create this elemental balance in your

earth, wind, fire, water, wood: the balanced garden

garden and see how every space now not only delights the eye but pleases all the senses.

The secret to styling successful gardens is to go one step at a time, and the five elements can serve as your guide. Here, I take one lackluster garden corner and bring it to life with five fun projects.

Water—As Many Styles as Fish in the Sea

In Zen philosophy, the element of water is a central metaphor for the natural flow of a well-lived life. Cultures the world over incorporate the look and sound of water, whether in the form of fountains or fish tanks, to add both energy and serenity to living spaces. Water can do the same for your backyard.

Wait, you may say, there's no stream ambling across my back lawn. They seem to have left out the duck pond when designing my backyard desert! At first glance, water features can seem difficult, even extravagant, but everyday styling makes it easy to bring this element onto your property. It may be a bubbler, fountain, or urn that you can create in a day, or a pond, pool, waterfall, riverbed, or water garden, which might take a little planning ahead. Whatever your pleasure, the power of water awaits you.

Styling supplies (can be found at most garden centers):

½ whiskey barrel

Plastic barrel liner

A bag of river rock

Fountain element (I used an old well pump)

Rebar for staking the fountain element (optional)

Fountain pump (size depends on how big your water feature will be)

½-inch thick-walled tubing for connections

• Place the barrel with the pump behind it. Cut the lip off the plastic liner and fit it into the barrel, ensuring that the top is below the rim. If you prefer not to use a liner, coat the barrel inside and out with a nontoxic water sealer instead.

• Fill the barrel one-third full with rock.

• For the fountain element, you can use just about anything that you can attach the tubing to or through; a watering can hanging from a tree above or even an old car part. For a well pump like I used here, drill a hole in the back close to the bottom. Use string or a wire coat hanger to feed the tubing through the hole you drilled up through the inner wall of the pump and out the front to the edge of the faucet. Petroleum jelly can be helpful to slide the tubing through. If necessary, secure the fountain element to the ground by staking it with rebar or digging it into the dirt.

• Place the fountain pump into the barrel, then take the tubing from the bottom end of the fountain element and attach it to the pump. Plug the pump into an outdoor-rated extension cord. (You can also opt for direct electrical wiring.) Fill the barrel with water from your hose and turn on the pump. The water will recycle itself, but watch for evaporation and refill as necessary.

Water Garden

Once you've got your water feature in place, why not add style with some plants? Aquatic plants can be an enigma to people more accustomed to gardening with those that grow in Mother Earth, but they're actually very easy to work with. These plants fall mainly into two groups: those that need to be rooted in a special aquatic soil mix and those that float. Here are some good picks from the world of water-based plant life.

• **Floating plants:** water hyacinth, water lettuce, duckweed, water soldier (an added advantage of floating plants is that they help to discourage algae)

• **Planted aquatics:** water lily, iris, yellow pond lily, sweet flag, flowering rush, horsetail

• **Oxygenators** (these absorb salts and release oxygen into the water): willow moss, water violet, water moss, water crowsfoot, curled pondweed

People in warm tropical regions, such as the southeast, enjoy the largest selection of water plants, while those on the West Coast have slightly fewer to choose from due to the winter chill. In very cold climates you're limited to grasses, which die in winter and come back the following year but you could try an indoor water garden in an enclosed porch or sunroom.

Earth—The Ground Beneath Your Feet

The way you choose to cover the earth affects the feel of any garden area, setting the tone from the ground up, so to speak. I love to build little patios out in the garden. The look adds variety, and the flat, dry surface offers a people-friendly oasis amid the plant life. For the patio in my elemental garden, I chose pink flagstone laid over pea gravel with river rock and blue star creeper filling in between the stones. Placing the patio next to the fountain makes this a natural spot for a seating area where people can relax and enjoy the soothing water sounds.

Style-to: Flagstone Patio

Styling supplies:

Pea gravel (enough to cover the area)

Dark pink flagstones

River rock (one large bag)

Blue star creeper (*Isotoma,* one flat)

- Mark out the area for your patio.
- Clear the area by removing the grass. I would normally do this before starting any work on the space.
- Remove any large roots and level the area.
- Spread pea gravel throughout the dirt area with a rake.
- Lay the flagstones onto the gravel, fitting the pieces together like a puzzle and leaving about an inch in between.
- If you need smaller pieces to make the puzzle fit together, use a mallet to break a piece of flagstone to size.
- Fill the gaps between with gravel, not quite up to the top of the flagstones.
- Add river rock on top of the gravel to create a level surface.
- For added style, plant blue star creeper or baby's tears around random pieces of flagstone.

patio and pathway plants

Planted accents can add a lot to a pathway or patio—a softening of the lines, a sense of history, a delicious scent. Good ground covers to plant between flagstones, bricks, or pavers include blue star creeper and baby's tears as well as herbs like thyme and oregano, which, when walked on, exude a lovely fragrance.

Wood—The Life of the Party

As the element that represents plant life, wood is all around in the garden. But with a whole world of plants to choose from, going beyond what's already growing in your garden can be an intimidating prospect. One good trick is to think of plants in palettes or groups that give certain looks and feels, just as you do colors or textures for indoor rooms.

Styling Tips

1 **Simple Plant Pleasures:** When choosing your plant palette, remember that less can be more for any given space. Pick just a few colors that work well together and harmonize—for instance, a grouping of soft pinks, whites, and lavenders. Or go bold with oranges, yellows, and reds. Blue and white also look beautiful together; you can add a piece of French pottery in the same tones as an accent.

2 **Plant Pointers:** Here are some plants from my garden makeover.

• **Delphinium**, or magic fountain, is a perennial that likes full sun and moderate to cooler zones. Easy to grow from seed, delphinium does need regular watering and fertilizing as well as protection from slugs and snails. It's very effective in borders, makes a good cut flower, and attracts birds with its pretty blossoms.

• **Verbena** is an easy-to-grow perennial that thrives in the heat and sun. It doesn't like to stay wet, so plant in an area that doesn't get too much water or move it to drier ground if you see signs of distress. My "patio hot pink" verbena is great for borders, containers, or hanging baskets because it will spread quickly and flower freely without any pinching, deadheading, or pruning.

• **Cosmos** likes full sun and can tolerate some aridity. It has a showy daisy-like flower in many colors that blooms in summer and fall, bringing in the birds. A free self-sower, cosmos is great for mass color in borders or backgrounds or as filler among shrubs.

Styling Tips

1 **Windmill:** Add a windmill to the garden to serve as a key focal point that spins around cheerily with each passing gust.

2 **Light Design:** Lights can make a design statement all their own. Try grouping three rod-mounted votive candleholders at different heights interspersed with the flowers in a garden bed. Other optical options include large candles, a canopy of small white twinkle lights hung from an arbor, or a chiminea.

Wind—Styling to Catch the Breeze

The breeze is the breath of life. How many times have you stepped outside a stuffy house or office to take a deep gulp of air, turning to meet the wind and letting it ruffle your hair? Fresh, circulating air carries oxygen, the most essential component of life (after chocolate), and it's a natural feature of your backyard. Why not style to showcase this element at its best?

The tricky thing about wind is that without a little human intervention, it's invisible. Enter everyday styling techniques that make wind's energy manifest to all those who gaze upon your garden.

Capturing the breeze with a pretty, fluttering flag is one way to keep things lively. Other breeze-catchers to consider include wind chimes, wind sockets, and umbrellas. Choose your own favorite fresh-air features—and don't forget to take a deep breath of garden air as a quick lift anytime.

Fire—Lighting to Create a Mood

Life in the garden doesn't end when the sun goes down. You'd never let your living room or dining room sink into darkness when evening falls, so don't forget lighting when you style your backyard. Just as the lamp at your front door welcomes people into your home at night, illumination in the backyard invites them out into your garden to enjoy the evening air. Fire is the element represented by backyard lighting features, and it comforts and inspires all who bask in its glow.

Begin with some strategically placed backyard basics such as a lantern positioned at the back fence, a fixture at the back door or patio, a garden spotlight at a cluster of trees. Dress up the look with candles, torches, strings of lights, hurricane lamps, or lanterns. There are many battery-powered outdoor lights and candle fixtures designed to protect the flame from the breeze, so don't let your electrical outlets limit your creative vision.

Style-to:
Espalier Climbing Roses

"Espalier" describes the practice of training trees, shrubs, or vines to grow flat against a wall or trellis. This process can take years, but my everyday espalier can be put into place on the spot to add color to a bare wall, or, in this case, a wood fence.

Styling supplies:

Drill
Screws
Screwdriver
White Banksian rose (A vigorous climber with rich green foliage and thornless slender branches that produces miniature white blooms that are quite profuse. Full sun. Grows 15–20 feet long. Zones 4–9.) Other options are:
• Etoile Violette clematis (Deep purple flowers. Zones 1–9. Full to partial sun.)
• "Blue Dawn" morning glory (Fast growing with large violet blue flowers. Zones 9–12. Full sun.)
• Showy jasmine (Small yellow flowers. Zones 4–9. Full sun.)
Monofilament fishing line (30-lb weight)
Floral tape

• Drill holes in the fence at 1-foot intervals, forming a zigzag pattern, and insert screws, leaving a bit of screw length exposed to hold the fishing line. Run the line up the fence, wrapping it around each screw to follow the zigzag design.
• Splay out the rose branches, weaving and twining them in and out of the fishing line to train.
• Attach the branches to the fishing line with floral tape.

nature goes mobile: styling with potted plants

Here's a great way to style unlikely garden spots, start developing your green thumb, or keep from getting stuck in the mud of traditional beds and borders: Make your plants mobile. Portable containers, whether antique or painted pots, hand-woven hanging baskets, or unexpected vessels like your punch bowl or casserole dish, offer endless creative opportunities for styling with things that grow. And best of all, each project is small and easy to achieve, no matter what your schedule or level of garden skills.

Potted plants are especially effective in areas with lots of concrete, or on decks, patios, porches, balconies, front entrances, and even on the grass. They add instant color and provide a focus for the eye. Pots can also make a fashion statement—like capping an outfit with the perfect hat—and because they're movable; you can change the look at will. Residents with small outdoor spaces may be limited entirely to pots, yet each container can be a compact mini-garden that expresses as much as a well-planted acre. Big yards also perk up with potted plants, as each different shape, size, color, and height adds texture and interest. The

designers of the great gardens of Versailles, summer home of the French kings and queens, used this same idea on a grand scale when they planted hundreds of orange trees in movable pots.

Tired of your backyard vista? There's no need to replant or wait for the next season when your plants are independently potted. Wishing for an upgrade to your urban view? Just place and group your self-contained beauties until you have the metropolitan garden of your dreams.

Everyday styling is meant to be easy and fun, so if fear of trowels and peat moss is keeping you cooped up inside, now's the time to get out into the sun! The perennial bed may be perennially on your to-do list, but you can get potting today.

pots on the spot

I don't know about you, but I like to strike when I'm hot on a project. So I keep a bunch of inexpensive small pots on hand for when I have a sudden yen to start a cutting, plant seeds with the kids, or try out a pilot plant in a certain area and see how it works before investing in a whole flat. I find that if the supplies aren't handy, the creative juices stop flowing and the moment slips away. A wood crate makes a great storage spot for spare pots, and helps to prevent any future creative leaks!

Style-to: Branch Wall Rack
Styling supplies:

14 3-foot-long branches (I gathered these on a hike)

Twine

Fresh or dried flowers

• Lay 12 branches on the ground horizontally, about an inch apart.

• Place the remaining 2 branches over the others on the perpendicular, about 3 inches in from each end. These are your vertical supports.

• Cut a piece of twine about 8–10 inches long and tie the first horizontal branch onto one of the vertical supports. Trim off the excess twine. Repeat for all the horizontal branches on both the vertical supports.

• Gently tie the flowers onto the horizontal branches. To hang, tie a piece of twine from one top back corner to the other and hang on a nail or screw.

Instant Potting Bench

Whether you have a green thumb or are completely green at gardening, you can easily set up a potting bench that has everything you need for styling with plants in one place. Dust off any old table, bench, or hutch lurking in your garage or spotted at the flea market and position it where you'd like to work. Next, pull together all your potting supplies—soil, pots, pruners, rakes, trowels, watering cans, garden clogs—and arrange them on and around your bench. Finally, surround your space with images that inspire your styling eye. I selected some plants I wanted to repot and a homemade branch rack for drying flowers.

A personalized potting bench can add a lovely garden flavor to any outdoor space and makes a stylish statement on side walls, bare patios, front or back porches, even apartment or condominium balconies.

Style-to: Branch Wall Rack

191

pots with patina

Why do some willingly pay a fortune for an old chipped table, aged chest, or a chair with cracked paint? Because such pieces have character and history, personality and style. Likewise, pots left out in the elements acquire a beautiful patina with age—but in this case the effect can easily be duplicated in an afternoon. There's nothing wrong with lending Mother Nature a helping hand!

Style-to: Paint-Aging Pots

Styling supplies:

Acrylic paints—titanium buff, turquoise, Hooker's green, and burnt umber

Paint mixing dish

Sea sponge

Terra-cotta pots

Water

Rubber gloves

• Squeeze a bit of each color into a dish.

• Wet sea sponge with water and wring out well. Choose a base color and lightly rub it on the pot, leaving some of the terra-cotta showing through. Paint the inside rim as well.

• Next dab on a second color, patting with your hand and fingers to blend as you go, or you can use a rag.

• Continue this process of layering until the desired result is achieved. Use the brown and the dark green under the lip and around the bottom for an aged moss look. The titanium buff color can be dabbed on here and there to simulate sodium water buildup.

Store-Bought Potting Bench

If you find you're potting a lot, you might consider moving on up to a specialized potting bench with spaces for tools, drawers for gloves, and storage below. Keep your bench freshly styled so that it invites and inspires your most illuminating ideas.

Styling Tip

1 **Bottle Rack Pot Holder:** I love using items in ways that weren't intended. When I found this old French bottle rack, I was quick to place pots where the bottles of Bordeaux used to go.

Whenever you see something eye-catching, stop for a moment to brainstorm different uses. For instance, my wine rack: I could hang ornaments on it at Christmas or twine lights around the pots. I might train some trailing ivy up through the rack to create a topiary. What about using it inside my studio to hold spools of twine and ribbon in many different colors?

Pots in a Rainbow of Colors

While the classic terra-cotta pot provides a neutral backdrop to show-case plants, you can also make pots part of your color palette. Whether you buy colored pots or add your own coat of paint, mix hues from across the spectrum or choose one to make a strong statement, pots in differ-ent colors can expand your rainbow of styling possibilities. Add annuals or perennials in complementary colors to bring sunshine to any outdoor space.

Styling Tips

1 **Pots in Unexpected Spots:** Don't limit yourself to the obvious when styling with potted plants. Sure, the patio and porch, driveway's edge, doorways, and balcony are good spots for pots, but you can add color to any part of the garden with potted plants.

2 **One Bright Pot:** Try placing just one brightly colored pot as a focal point, surrounded by a sprinkling of river rock.

3 **Pot Tree:** For an everyday antidote to a boring bare wall, ex-plore the many innovative items available to add plant power, from lattices to trellises, hangers, and hooks. This pot tree filled with colorful annuals brings vertical dimension and a prismatic palette to an otherwise dull back wall.

Style-to: Four Steps to Simple Potting

To pot any plant for a long and healthy life, follow four simple steps:

1. Fill the bottom of the pot with gravel or terra-cotta chips for drainage, to prevent the plant's roots from getting waterlogged and rotted.

2. Add fresh potting soil to the pot, leaving room for the root ball and some attached dirt. It's important to use new soil rather than dirt from the yard, as purchased potting soil is free from disease and fortified with key nutrients.

3. Remove the plant from its plastic pot, loosen the dirt around the root ball, and place it in the pot.

4. Cover the roots with enough dirt to fill the pot up to 1–2 inches from the top depending on its size (you want to leave some room here to prevent dirt overflow when watering). Gently pack the soil to hold the plant upright, and water.

kid-friendly potting

Children love to pot, and it's a chance for them to learn about the natural world while they get their hands in the dirt. Hutton is my favorite garden helper, and he has a great time digging as well as deciding which combination of plants and pots to use.

To get your kids potting, let them help you paint or age the pots first (use a nontoxic water-based paint), then show them the four basic potting steps above. Give them some annuals to work with and let them go to town.

Just like us, kids learn best by doing, and the sooner they connect with the earth the deeper their lifelong bond to Mother Nature's beauty may be. And wait until you see their pride in their works of living art!

bringing it all together:
one-day garden makeover

Although I hadn't planned to do a complete garden makeover for this book (I was saving them for the next book) as I was racing to meet the publisher's deadline, I realized that if I didn't include one here I'd be holding out on you. Besides, I was itching to get a hold of my friends' backyard and this was the perfect opportunity. Soon I was off to a full one-day garden makeover (the kind I'm so used to) that would bring together all the styling ideas I've described throughout the outdoor section—inviting entryways, lovely and functional outdoor rooms, gardens that tap the full beauty of nature's elements.

This backyard had a lovely lawn, but my homeowners felt that overall it lacked charm and character. "It's just boring," said my friends. "The kids play out there, but we never invite guests. The garage wall is chipped, the plants are struggling, and we have no place to entertain." With the challenge on the table I sat down to design the yard. I wanted color, fun, defined spaces for parties, play, and hanging out every day. Coming up: a yard they would be proud of!

By following the basics in this section and trying the styling tips and style-to's (or your own variations), you too can transform your yard, taking it just one step at a time. Want some company while you style? Try recruiting your family and neighbors to form your own green team!

before

197

color for contrast or camouflage

If your background wall has existing windows or doors, decide whether to draw attention to them or make them disappear. You can accent features by painting them a color that contrasts with the wall or use the same color for camouflage. I chose a yellow for my wall color and a dusty purple-blue to accentuate the shutters and door against the yellow. I love the look of age in the garden, and a great way to get it is with lime-wash paint (see resources). Correctly applied, lime-wash gives a natural aged nuance to the humblest garage wall.

Spotlighting a Garage Wall

Many people have a plain garage wall serving as the side of their yard, as did my homeowners here. Though you might wish it would just go away, a wall can actually be a wonderful canvas upon which to style. Any wall looks more inviting when it has an entryway, even if it's false. *Trompe l'oeil* is the technical term for faux architecture, and you can use this trick to turn a plain wall into a marvelous mystery.

To bring a sense of sun and fun to this space, I painted the wall yellow, then played up the window with shutters and added a mirrored door to create a faux entryway. With the background in place, the next step was to add a seating area with a bench, bright flowerpots that echo the blue and yellow color scheme, and a birdbath to attract feathered friends. A curved gravel walkway carves out the planting beds to complete the tableau.

Styling Tips

1 **Color Coordinated Bench:** An ordinary bench becomes a stylish seating area when you put color to work. Take an old bench or purchase a new one and paint it the color of your background wall or trim. Enhance this outdoor room by adding flowerpots in your color palette to tie it all together.

2 ***Trompe l'oeil* Entrance:** Search the garage, basement, and flea markets for shutters and doors to create your *trompe l'oeil* entrance. I found this old mirrored door at a salvage yard, while the

shutters were hidden in the homeowner's basement. If you don't have a window, add one and rag on some paint over the panes so that it looks aged and no one will ever know that it's not real. Hang shutters and doors using molly bolts and a power drill.

Finish with a front stoop made simply by laying used bricks over gravel in a basket weave pattern.

So, you've decided it's time for a paint job to perk up a space. How do you get started?

First check your Style File for the colors you like in the area you're preparing to paint. Pull out all the tear sheets that catch your eye, then narrow the choices with this paint board technique.

Style-to: Paint Boards

One of the primary challenges when it's time to paint is choosing the right colors, and that requires seeing the paint as it will really look in a big, uninterrupted swatch. The solution? Paint boards.

Styling supplies:

Foam core boards
Paint in the colors you're considering
Paintbrushes and cleanup supplies

• Purchase one large foam core board for each color on your list from your local art supply store. I prefer foam core to poster board, though it may be a few dollars more, because it stands up against the wall so you can stand back and judge.

• Paint each board in one of the colors you're considering for the space and let dry.

• Place your paint boards against the wall, trying different pairings until you find the one or combination that works for you. Don't be limited by conventional choices.

Paint boards are just as useful inside the house as out, and you can make them up in several different colors and move them from room to room as your styling process evolves.

Play with color in the garden. Bring it up out of your plants and splash it on the walls. Style transcends the earthbound categories of terra firma!

bring on the birds

Birds bring life to the garden. But how do you bring them in? Offer them what they need: water (a birdbath), food (a bird feeder), and shelter (a birdhouse), and of course the right plant material (shrubs and trees for nesting and colorful plants to nourish them with their nutritious seeds and nectar). Whether you hang a birdhouse in a tree, perch it on top of a wood post, or attach it to a fence, meeting birds' wants and needs can attract your personal aviary.

Outdoor Entertaining for Grownups and Kids

This yard lacked the most basic space required by social animals like us: an entertainment area. To define this outdoor room I looked both to the ground and the sky: I created a quick mortarless patio underfoot and put up a canvas pergola overhead. After removing the existing grass and putting down a layer of gravel, I dusted off a bunch of old brick that was lying in a corner of the yard and nestled it in. Patio, done. For the pergola, a painter's cloth painted yellow, four posts, and a bit of knot work did the job. I added a table and chairs for al fresco dining and lanterns to light the way. The final step was a children's area with a set of pint-size furniture.

When it's not rough-and-tumble time, children love to sit outside to draw, read, or have a little tea party. I created this quiet-time outdoor room to give the kids a place to be and add whimsy to the overall look of the yard. Stenciled paint adds personality to any old or unfinished table; this mini model came in a kit. Why not let the kids do the stenciling with a little supervision while you're painting your wall?

Style-to: Stenciled Table and Chairs

Styling supplies:

Children's table and chair set
Paint in two complementary colors
    plus additional colors for stenciling
Paintbrushes
Stencil
Small sea sponge
Dish of water
Cleanup supplies

• Paint the table one solid color and the chairs another color that contrasts well. Let dry.
• Pour your stenciling paint into small dishes. Position the stencil on the table. Wet the sea sponge with a little water to soften, dip the edge into the paint, and sponge lightly over the stencil. Work from the middle toward the outer edges so that you don't find yourself leaning across wet paint. Continue with as many colors as you like. Don't apply the paint too heavily or it will bleed through the stencil.
• Gently lift off the stencil and let the paint dry.

Style-to: Instant Brick and Gravel Patio

Styling supplies:

Shovel
Gravel (regular or pea), enough to lay a
    2- to 3-inch base and fill in the
    cracks between bricks
Bricks, enough to cover the patio area

• Mark off your patio area and dig up the grass, removing any large rocks and roots.
• Spread a layer of gravel about 2–3 inches thick as a base to completely cover the area.
• Lay the bricks in a basketweave pattern of perpendicular pairs.
• Spread more gravel between the bricks to fill in the gaps and create a flat, even surface.

Character and charm are always in arm's

Styling Tips

1 **Canvas Pergola:** Put a roof over your head with a pergola—a.k.a. an awning draped over four posts—to provide shade and define your entertaining space. To make one you'll need to sink four posts at the corners of your patio, anchored either in concrete or in post stakes with additional anchor stakes. Then stretch rope between the posts to form an X, lay a canvas over the rope and tie it to the top of the posts and then down to the anchor posts. I used a painter's cloth painted yellow to create a sunny "sky" and pick up the color scheme of the garage wall.

2 **Double-Duty Birdbath:** A birdbath plays two roles in the garden: It looks great and also serves as a beacon to attract our feathered friends. Place it in amongst the flowers, or stand it alone as a main attraction.

202

reach when you take one simple step at a time.

3 **Plants on Many Planes:** Just like they used to line the kids up by height at school, you want to put taller plants in the back of the bed and work your way forward as they get shorter. In this garden I wanted a feel of the south of France, so I filled it with tones of blue, yellow, and white. My annual-perennial mix includes: **Delphinium "Magic Fountain"**—large stalks with small flowers; **Happy Returns Daylily**—beautiful stalks with large yellow flowers. Zones 1–12; **Alyssum**—mounds of tiny fragrant flowers; **First Love Gardenia**—beautiful double blooms are larger than any other gardenia. Zones 8–11; **Silvery Sunproof Lilyturf**—beautiful variegated foliage with spikes of soft lilac flowers. Zones 1–12. Great for borders; **Calendula**—bright yellow and orange flowers over a very long season; **Royal Cape Plumbago**—huge clusters of vivid blue flowers cover this shrub most of the year. Zones 9–11.

confidence and creativity

I may be a lifestylist, but to my family I'm Mom or Honey and I don't have carte blanche to do whatever I want with the house or garden. Like you, I have to take everyone's needs into consideration.

With that said, I can't overemphasize how important it is not to censor the creative process when you style. Don't let friends or family stop you as you search for your own sensibilities. Here are some principles of free expression to keep in mind:

• Ask the people in your life for support. If they start to shoot you down, challenge them to build on your idea instead.

• Find a Style File buddy you can talk to when everyone else thinks you've lost your mind.

• Remember that it can be hard for others to see your vision until it's done, so don't be swayed by interim opinions. Pursue your own creative process until you get the result you want.

• If someone doesn't love something you've finished, try to be objective about their comments and see if it can be improved upon.

• Finally, make sure to maintain a sense of humor about it all.

True creativity requires taking risks, even failing from time to time. Censorship is creativity's enemy. Say no to "no," and let your creative juices flow!

Whenever my creative spirit flags, I go out into the garden. I might work on something—pulling weeds, repotting plants, playing with my accents and accessories—or I may just sit, stealing a moment of quiet. In either case, I take advantage of the opportunity to meditate upon a simple truth: A plant has no choice but to grow. As soon as it stops synthesizing sunlight into food and reaching its roots and leaves farther out into the world, the plant dies. Yes, some species go dormant through the winter, but the first rays of spring sun summon them back to blossom.

To me, a plant epitomizes the creative spirit. My garden helps me to tap this energy even when my schedule seems impossible or I feel frustrated, uncertain, or stopped. Inspired by the vital example of nature, I get back to the business of making every moment beautiful for me and those I love. Some people talk to their plants, but I mostly listen. What they say is, "Keep creating . . . that's the joy of life."

susie's favorite resources

Indoors

American Folk & Fabric, Inc.
626-358-7111
www.americanfolkandfabric.com
Offers reproductions of authentic
vintage and antique linens.

Anthropologie
800-309-2500
www.anthropologie.com
An original mix of accessories,
furniture, and gifts.

Authentico
310-558-3661
Custom furniture in Los Angeles.

Cost Plus World Market
800-COST-PLUS
www.costplusworldmarket.com
Unique treasures from around the world.

Crate & Barrel
800-996-9960
www.crateandbarrel.com
Great seasonal items and basics for
every room of your home.

Department 56
800-548-8696
www.D56.com
Seasonal accessories and collectibles.

John Roberts Floriculturist
818-790-0733
no Web site
Home and garden accessories store
in La Cañada, California.

Kristal
800-766-2425
www.kristal.com
A complete line of personal products,
candles, and home accessories.

Mecca
626-577-0012
www.meccastudio.com
Custom invitations, gift items, and all
bridal needs in Pasadena, California.

Pier1 imports
800-295-4595
www.pier1.com
Wonderful imports for home and garden.

Pottery Barn
800-922-5507
www.potterybarn.com
Great linens, pillows, accessories, and
seasonal items for the home.

Restoration Hardware
888-243-9720
www.restorationhardware.com
High-quality furniture, lighting, hardware,
and discovery items.

Sur La Table
800-243-0852
www.surlatable.com
Beautiful French table linens, dishes,
and cookware.

Target
800-800-8800
www.target.com
The hottest trend merchandise and everyday
basics at affordable prices for your home.

The Antique House
818-790-1119
www.hometown.aol.com/antekhaus/index.htm
Antique furniture, art, and furnishings from
the 18th through the early 20th century.

Outdoors

Al's Garden Art
909-424-0221
www.alsgardenart.com
Fountains, planters, and other cast stone merchandise.
Provided birdbaths, pots, and garden art.

Beckett Corporation
972-871-8000
www.beckettpumps.com
Water gardening supplies.

Color Spot Nurseries
800-554-4065
www.colorspot.com
A fantastic wholesale nursery offering everything
from quality bedding plants to Christmas trees.
Supplied all of the annuals in the book.

Dan Weedon Landscape Architect
310-827-2084
Great landscape architect.

Garden
818-788-3400
www.garden-thestore.com
Unique garden accessories.

Gardeners Eden
800-822-9600
www.gardenerseden.com
Decorative indoor furniture, floral, and lighting.
Provided a variety of garden accessories, trellises,
and watering cans.

International Market Gallery
650-952-0525
www.cityspin.com/sanfrancisco/shopping/edits/e809int0.htm
Ethnic rugs, pottery, and furniture.

Lime Wash Pots
323-665-0823
www.limewashpots.com
Italian terra-cotta pots painted in authentic lime wash.

Lowe's
800-44-LOWES
www.lowes.com
Great selection of items for all home and
garden needs. Very consumer friendly!

Monrovia Nursery
800-PLANT-IT
www.monrovia.com
One of the world's largest producers of
container-grown plants. Supplied all the perennials
and trees used in this book.

Orchard Supply Hardware
888-746-7674
www.osh.com
Wonderful store—easy to shop for all home
and garden improvement items.

QVC
800-345-1515
www.qvc.com
The number-one televised shopping service also
has a great Web site with a wide variety of products
for home, garden, and entertaining.

Scavenger's Paradise
323-877-7945
www.scavengersparadise.com
Sells, rents, and buys architectural elements.

Schultz
314-298-2700
www.schultz.com
Home and garden care equipment.

Sears Hardware
800-4-MY-HOME
www.sears.com
For your home improvement needs. Great tools!

Smith & Hawken
800-776-3336
www.smithandhawken.com
Great garden tools and accessories.
Beautiful pots and vases.

Sydney Harbour Paint Company
818-623-9394
www.sydneyharbourpaintco.com
Stocks a variety of paint products that
are great for special finishes. Provided
lime wash paint for garden walls.

acknowledgments

A zillion thanks from the bottom of my heart for the love, sacrifice, support, and fun all of you gave to this book . . .

Erinn Valencich, my assistant and friend. Words cannot express how grateful I am. I never could have done this without you. I love your enthusiasm and your willingness to tackle anything! I admire you so much.

Michael Broussard, my agent and dear friend—you are a ball of fire. I love your energy, determination, and tenacity. Thank you for your incredible contributions and support. Thank you, Jan Miller, *agent extraordinaire,* for encouraging me to write my first lifestyle book and selling it in true Miller fashion.

The team at Simon & Schuster: My publisher, David Rosenthal, vice president, and deputy publisher, Walter Weintz. The marketing, sales, and publicity teams—you came through with everything you promised and more. Also to Constance Herndon who bought the book and Amanda Murray who took it to the finish line.

Jenny Barry—for your wonderful talent and bringing to bear the wisdom of your previous two hundred illustrated books, and most of all for understanding my vision and translating it into this book. You are a true artist.

My talented crew: Jennifer Cheung and Steven Nilsson; Michele Adams, Sue Hudelson-Leland, Haijun Park, Suzi Smitts, Mary O'Grady, Ken Hellenbolt, and Dan Weedon—all of you helped to materialize my vision.

My indispensable associates: Elizabeth Miles, for all of your guidance and contribution with the manuscript; your love, support, and positive energy inspired me to stay true to my vision. Peter Gelfan for being there whenever I needed you. You have great talent and insight. Thanks for your editorial contribution. And to Susan La Tempa for your excellent input.

My *Surprise Gardener* producers, Tito Romero, Gary Bernstein, and Steve Radosh, and my HGTV executives, Burton Jablin, Michael Dingley, and Scripps Networks CEO and chairman, Ken Lowe, for your continued support: it's been a wonderful ride working with all of you and being part of this terrific network. Jeff Zucker, Linda Finnell, and Betsy Alexander of NBC for signing me to the *Today* show. Stewart Weiner of *Palm Springs Life* magazine for being one of the first to put me into print with my own column. I am forever grateful for these wonderful opportunities to work with the best in the business!

The many fans, adults as well as children, who have e-mailed me, written, come to see me at appearances or watched me on TV—without you and your support there wouldn't be any of this! From the bottom of my heart I am thankful to each and every one of you for helping to make every day a joyous one, as I love what I do.

This book and my career would not have been possible without all the love and support I get at home: Eva Mazzariegos, who for the last seven years has cared not only for my house and children but also for me—thank you. My mother-in-law, Cally Vickers: you have been a second mom to me; thank you for your enthusiasm, interest, and encouragement. Angelica Holiday for believing in me from the start and never giving up—you are amazing! Kristin Menschik for your many years of dedication, and Kathryn Parten for all your help. And all of my friends, you know who you are, without your love and late-night calls I would have felt alone in the process. Thanks for sharing the experience with me.

And especially to Bobby, Hutton, and Hailey for understanding my time away and my late nights writing, for your constant (if sometimes inadvertent) inspiration, and for making it all worthwhile. I love you more than I can express.